Resurgent India

By the same author

—., History of the Punjabees

—., Human Eternity : Stone Age to Mustopia

—., Bengal : The Unique State

—., Religion and Philosophy for Modern Youth

—., Development of the Resources to the Sea : India

—., Science and Technology in Indian Transformation.

About the Authors

Prof. J.N. Nanda besides being an "Eminent Scientist" with two earned doctorates in Physics and Applied Physics respectively has also been active in the social and cultural sphere. He was the first scientist in India to begin research work in oceanography and underwater sound. He prefers the advance of co-existence rather than aiming at "unity in diversity". Understanding the complexity of human mind, he advocates a new Mahayana of co-existence and earnest efforts to square beliefs with advances in science and technology. He has numerous papers and books to his name. He has travelled extensively and led some government delegations abroad.

M.S Batra, M.A. (Economics), LL. B., retired as Deputy Director General, All India, Radio. He was earlier Head of the Lucknow and Delhi Stations of AIR. During his service, he was deputed on a Government of India Fellowship to Kabul University for advanced studies in the Pashto language. He evolved into a renowned Pashto scholar and an expert on Afghan affairs. He worked as Programme Adviser and Secretary to the Punjabi Academy of the Government of NCT, Delhi. He produced innumerable programmes and wrote commentaries on international affairs for broadcast on All India Radio. He is a keen student of India's relations with other countries and the world scene, besides being Honorary Editor of a magazine relating to comparative religions.

RESURGENT INDIA

J.N. Nanda

M.S. Batra

CONCEPT PUBLISHING COMPANY PVT. LTD.
NEW DELHI-110059

ISBN-13-978-81-8069-709-8

First Published 2011

Printed and Published by

Concept
Since 1974

Concept Publishing Company Pvt. Ltd.
Regd. Office:
A/15-16, Commercial Block, Mohan Garden
New Delhi-110059 (India)
Phones : 25351460, 25351794, *Fax* : 091-11-25357109
Email : publishing@conceptpub.com
Website: www.conceptpub.com

Editorial Office:
H-13, Bali Nagar, New Delhi-110 015, India.

Cataloging in Publication Data--*Courtesy:* D.K. Agencies (P) Ltd. <docinfo@dkagencies.com>

Nanda, J. N., 1920-
Resurgent India / J.N. Nanda, M.S. Batra.
p. cm.
Includes index.
ISBN 9788180697098

1. India--Politics and government. 2. India--Foreign relations. 3. India--Economic policy. I. Batra, M. S., joint author. II. Title.

DDC 320.954 22

Dedication in Nehru's Words

Our Final aim can only be a Classless
Society with equal Economic Justice
and Opportunity for all, a Society
for the Raising of Mankind to a
Cultivation of Spiritual Values
of Cooperation, Unselfishness,
the spirit of Science, the
Desire to do Right,
Goodwill and Love,
Ultimately
a World
Order

PREFACE

Resurgence of a peace loving India means, among other things, its recapture of the same status as a travel destination as it had in its golden age. India's significance was due to the esteem it inspired and the reputation it enjoyed for its advancement and riches. For a thousand years before the Hun explosion over the known world, Indian teachers and preachers, medical practitioners and merchants had roamed to China and Byzantine in peace and welcome. A Buddhist empire extended from India to Palestine for two centuries around the birth of Christ. India was the holy land for Hindu-Buddhist scholars who flocked to Indian universities in Kashmir or Bihar. Indian temple architecture had spread in East Asia. Indian arts and crafts were flooding the Indian markets with products of the potter's wheel and household looms for luring the European gold and silver. India was the trade hub between Europe and Asia. A branch of the silk route to China passed through India.

The resurgence of India stands for its regaining the ancient position for being the centre of arts and sciences, and a nation with well-earned reputation of being endowed with good mercantile culture. India has made strides to gain its deserved position among the trading nations of the world. Its economy is booming and it has been steadily attracting foreign investments. There is considerable competence in the manufacture of engineering goods and growth of electronic industry including computer hardware and software. India has a thriving industry of oil refining and expertise in sustainable energy resources. The present globalization has found in it a natural swimmer. India has vigorously pursued the nuclear treaty with USA which may materialise, if our internal politics permit, and it would augment our power production and export earnings by having a share in nuclear reactor trade.

India will be a partner with all nations for peace. India's

proposals for disarmament are highly comprehensive and certain to be eventually accepted by the world. India is for revision of the UN charter and change in the veto provisions as well as modification of the CTBT and the non-proliferation treaty so that all countries can subscribe to these without reservations. India has made strides in bio-technology, nano-technology and production of nuclear energy. Indian knowledge and experience are readily available to all countries without any strings attached. India is already the chosen country for many tourist programmes and it is vigorously improving the communication network in the country.

This book covers the resurgence of India in some fields, like sustainable development, democratic decision-making, public health, and intensive utilization of sunshine, combating terrorism and exploitation. India's foreign policy postures are discussed in detail. We hope to see India shed poverty and to be in the forefront of nations with gender equality.

Contents

1 Introduction and Prologue

1.1 World Peace

Starting from tribal anarchy, the world reached anarchy among nations in the nineteenth century. A push towards a peaceful united world was visible after the world wars in the twentieth century. Memories of exclusive greatness were still alive particularly in the USA and the ex-imperialist nations of the West as well as the East. The invention and the employment of the atom bomb and subsequent economic and monetary strength brought about the political situation to be that of a uni-polar world with USA as a visible single pole. Even if looking at the century long opposition from South America, USA gives up any imperialist domination of the western hemisphere, it still has to ensure its dominant position in the world by enforcing the acceptance by the majority of nations the same economic and political views as held by the USA. These problems are a legacy of the imperialist past of UK and France who are now powerful states on the side of the USA. Russia, Japan and Germany hope to dedicate themselves to rebuilding their strength to win their deserved status. China and India have confidence in their task of bringing prosperity to their enormous population when so many Chinese and Indians are living at or below subsistence levels. For most of the world, continued absence of wars and world peace are essential.

1.2 Role of India

India is a large country sheltering about one-sixth of the world population. It has naturally an important role in ensuring world peace and has given many demonstrations of its inclination towards separating antagonists and supporting the peaceful solution of disputes. It is on account of visible peace initiatives of India that so many countries both of the first world and the second world rallied to India's side for calling on China to desist from further damage to India and India-China friendly relations when the Chinese out of their own feeling of insecurity attacked India in the sixties aligning themselves to Pakistan specifically created by the imperialists to put brakes on India's growing propensity to lay down decorum in international affairs even for stronger countries. How does India manage to fearlessly espouse the right action to nations? Very often it is because, out of long suffering, India has learnt to have great sympathy for the common people of the world, who often suffer from the ambitions of ruling classes or faults of capitalism, communism, fascism or fanaticism in their own country or in a foreign country. In trying to fathom the ancient and modern sources of the Indian stance, we shall first trace the growth of Indian culture and India's evolution into a secular democratic state pursuing mixed economy and marching towards the goal of internal and external peaceful coexistence. Next, we shall examine India's apparent dual role as a nuclear power and its firm commitment to nuclear disarmament, India's struggle to industrialize and efforts to gain economic strength as well as persistence in welfare economics notwithstanding heavy burden of contending against a plethora of gifted armaments in its neighbourhood. India does not believe in military alliances. It has opted for transparency and resolution of conflicts by democratic discussions in the wider interests of human civilization. Before we deal with the growth of modern Indian nation and her policies for economic strength and the welfare of the Indian people, we shall trace in a brief prologue, the ups and downs of the Indian civilization till 1919 A.D. It is the massacre at Jallianwala in Amritsar in 1919 A.D. that gave a fillip to the struggle for Indian independence from the British colonial rule.

1.3 Prologue

(i) India in 1500 B.C.

The Indian civilization must have had its beginning as far back as other ancient civilizations: China, Egypt and Sumeria. All these ancient civilizations have left records of their commerce and trade with India. India was populated by native tribes from stone age and by arrivals from China, the Kabul river valley, or from northern heights broken by many river valleys. The nearest civilized settlements were in Iran and the Iranians gave the name Hindu Kush to the mountain ranges north of the Kabul river. The word Hindu had stuck to the inhabitants of the Kabul river valley and later to all others to the east. Speech and language were the first signs of civilized life followed by the use of tools and the development of knowledge of primitive agriculture, raising of herds of sheep or cattle. Superstition and leadership of clever tribal chiefs gave rise to tribal religious observances and temporal relations (based on chance) with observation of stars in the sky, led to religion. Religion tried to satisfy the human curiosity about the first causes and together with poetry and philosophy, religious compositions became common even without the aid of writing. Writing was invented primarily for commerce and the religious compositions taught from memory came later to be committed to writing. India had a flux of tribes who were also cattle herders and fought from horse drawn chariots. They called themselves Aryans and the Vedas composed before 1500 B.C. in the region of the Punjab and Kashmir were regarded as their sacred books. The Hindus of India, a mixed lot of inhabitants of India within the geographical limits set by the Himalayas in the north, Indian Ocean in the south and Himalayan offshoots in the east and the west gave them the feeling of having a special home endowed with all natural blessings and they started worshipping the habitat in their prayers. Their religion included worship of Siva with chief centre of worship at Varanasi and also particular worship of fauna and flora popular to Siva in

Sind and in the forests all over the country along with that of the mother goddess or the spouse of Siva. The co-existence of many kinds of worship among the Hindus made them catholic and tolerant in their intercourse with others and made them receptive to new ideas which is now a characteristic of Indians in all walks of life. 1500 B.C. is regarded as a turning point in Indian history. It was about then that the *Mahabharata* civil war took place at Kurukshetra in the Punjab where contingents from all over India took part. The war ended in the victory of the faction led by Krishna, whom the grateful victorious forces raised to the level of God incarnate and a beautiful religious poem *Gita* ascribed to Krishna gives the sum total of the Hindu philosophy as to live performing one's duty and seeing equality in all faiths. Vyas, the chronicler of *Mahabharata* has included in his poetic composition almost all the extant gems of Indian poetic literature of his day and most Indians as well as people of East Indies and West Asia who were in contact with Hindu traders and travellers cherish this cultural treasure house. In those days it is clear that politically small kingdoms existed in the entire country and each king felt it to be his domain. The inhabitants of India idolized their country. Various chiefs started setting up new settlements in the surrounding forests or forcing other kings to accept vassalage. The important seats were at Multan, Delhi, Srinagar, Kashi, Assam, Manipur, Puri, Magadh, Tamralipti, Calicut. The soldiers fought with weapons of copper and iron or with maces, stones or bows and arrows. The ancient Chinese developed gunpowder but used it only for festivities. The Indians did not use any firearms. In their mythical descriptions of godly weapons, however, they described their effects practically like the effects of ABC weapons. Travel by boat on the inland waterways and on small ships hugging the coasts had become common.

(ii) India in 500 B.C.

These kingdoms and small republics were all very loyal to their kings or governing councils but they, on the whole, followed common sacred traditions of behaviour of individuals and states. Village councils, guilds of technicians, residential schools for children in the homes or villages of teachers, places of worship of mother goddess, Siva, or of Aryan sacrifice of sweet smelling herbs and butter oil in fire apportioned to various Vedic deities existed in abundance. The people had a sense of well-being and could practice charity, go on pilgrimages and take part in community discussions and attend to the needs of travellers and Brahmans who tried to live to teach, meditate and preserve traditions. Since most knowledge and skills had to be learnt at home, professional castes were emerging. Expansion and amalgamation of certain teachers' schools formed universities often liberally supported by people and ruling houses. Free discussions and meditation led to the formation of many philosophies both theistic and atheistic. The Buddha and Mahavira had laboured a century earlier. As a student can change his chosen field and teacher in an American university, an Indian could with complete liberty change his adherence to a new philosophical system or new religious rituals. All believed in everlasting soul, its transmigration and rebirth and human beings to be bound to the law of *karma, i.e.* as you sow so shall you reap in the current or in a future life. Important religious and medicine related books had been written. *Manu Smriti*, rules for Sanskrit language, logic and texts of daily prayers had been composed.

An empire (Nanda dynasty) with capital at Patliputra was established. There was an Ikshwaku dynasty ruled from Nagarjunkonda in Andhra. A business of common people was to attend debates and discourses and express their acceptance or rejection of propositions expounded by the learned people. People were prone to apply their minds to all kinds of problems like efficacy of sacrifices authorized by the Brahmans, or supremacy of non-violence as made popular by Buddhists and Jains. Whatever one's mode of prayer, the middle path of the Buddha appealed most to reason. China had erected its Great Wall and debated incessantly on good manners and invented periodical examinations in philosophy for selecting their rulers. Iran became an imperial power and Alexander was to set out to conquer the world after briefly tasting imperial power in Iran a century later when his Greek armies conquered Iran.

India had surplus production of sugar, rice, pottery products, cowries as universal coinage, salt, gold and silver ornaments, hand tools, cotton wear etc. and traded with many countries by sea or *via* caravan routes. Indian scholars, priests, lecturers and merchants roamed the world in search of pupils and wealth especially in the East Indies and in Turkestan. Indian destinations had also become important because of the teachings of the Buddha and Mahavira and the existence of many renowned teachers especially for Sanskrit, Astronomy, and Jyotish (Astrology). It is a mistake to distinguish too much between Buddhism and Hinduism. Any one could show preference to one system or the other without any sense of religious conversion. Hindu or Buddhist scholars had often the same patrons and lived and meditated at the same place. There was simultaneous spread of Shaivite Hinduism, Buddhism, Shakti cults and common man's *bhakti* and faith in miracles.

(iii) India (500 B.C. to 1857 A.D.)

Alexander's incursion into India provoked this country to attend to statecraft and learn developments outside India. The Greek forces encamped with cooperating Indian rulers were eliminated within a decade and a second Greek invasion (now by Alexander's Asian satrap Seleucus) was overcome by Chandragupta Maurya, the head of the Maurya dynasty which succeeded the Nanda dynasty. Megasthenes, the ambassador of Seleucus stationed at Patliputra, has written a glowing account of the Indian capital and the Indian system of government, an important feature of which was the secret service particularly on the ferreting out of economic and security offences.

A Buddhist empire with capital at Peshawar (now in Pakistan) extended from there to limits of West Asia for a couple of centuries and later Manicheism (a syncretic religion based on Indian, Christian and Zoroastrian beliefs) evolved in western Iran and spread throughout the territories occupied by the Buddhist empire in the second century A.D. It is forgotten now in most of the region but for some remnants in the Himachal Pradesh state of India where still exist some Hindu temples dedicated to worship of fire from the ignition of some gas that issues forth from Earth's interior. Iran had felt some right of conquest in the area overrun by Greek-Iran army of Alexander extending to practically entire present day Pakistan. West Punjab was often a province of Iran, Baghdad caliphate or the Afghan expansion into India.

Throughout the past all the major countries of the world or rather the continental regions, China, East Asia , India, Iran, West Asia, Europe and North Africa had inter-regional trade usually indirect through coastal or caravan halting stations. Indian ports in Saurashtra, Andhra and Bengal were very active and so were the caravan route access stations in Punjab like Multan, Mansehra, Jhelum, Kabul, Peshawar and Poonchh. Indian princes of large or small principalities though endeavoured to enlarge their boundaries, yet there seemed to be no wish to add to India any foreign territory by conquest. The Indian geography and relatively poor quality agricultural land across Indian boundaries was discouraging for any foreign adventures, but the Indian self-satisfaction in the security of their village society was rudely jolted by the appearance of Alexander's conquering armies across the Jhelum river in 326 B.C. The only state directly under threat was Punjab ruled by Porus. He had no one else to stand by him and on his defeat the whole of India was open to Alexander's advance, but Porus had demonstrated the prowess of Indian defence and Alexander won him over by restoring his kingdom to him. Alexander's troops refused to go further into India having heard of the immense strength of the ruler of the East (Assam and Bengal) and Alexander decided to return to Iran.

In 500 A.D. India was in the middle of its golden age. There was intellectual contact with Greece, Iran and China. The third Buddhist Council had adopted the advances to Mahayana, thus opening the opportunity for all to come in the orbit of Hindu-Buddhism. Indian teachers and traders roamed all over Asia and Indian colonies came to exist in every country, influencing the culture and life style in all countries. Indian physicians were held in high esteem. India exported metal-ware, pottery, sugar, salt, jute and cotton. Indians earned the reputation of honesty in their commercial undertakings. Peace and order existed throughout the land. The noble heroism of the epics and devotion to feudal duties was widespread. The writings of the Chinese scholars who visited the Indian centres of sanctity and power in the beginning and towards the end of the golden age extol the achievements of the Indians in literature, philosophy and sciences. Dhanvantri Nighantu written in that period gives the description and medicinal use of many herbs and roots. There is the mention of 362 arts practiced by people during the golden age period. Iron chains and nails were in common use. India's export trade brought in considerable wealth in gold and silver. Roman gold coins are still being unearthed from many sites in India.

Buddhism had dwelt on ethical action and no reliance on miraculous support from God. The Buddhists started praying to his statues and then began following Mahayana, little different from Hinduism. India became abuzz with worship of Rama and Krishna. The philosophical underpinning to all religious thought of India was provided by the *Gita* and the zeal of Adi Shankaracharya of Kerala who won debates in all corners of India.

The Pallava dynasty of South India flourished at Mallapuram in South India from 100 A.D. to 900 A.D. They built magnificent monuments with designs that were a precursor of Ajanta and Ellora.

The Buddhist states along the Indus and the Oxus were soon overrun by Islam and the public converted to Islam which had no intermediary priestly class. A simplistic faith was also spread that the wealth accumulated by non-believers was legitimately the property reserved by God for the believers. This teaching was interpreted by many as a licence for despoiling the non-believers. The ethnic clearance perpetrated by Muslim League zealots in the Muslim majority border areas starting with Kohat in the period between the two World Wars resulted in expulsion of Hindus and Sikhs, bereft of any valuables, to seek fortune in Muslim minority areas of India. Even the Kashmiri Pandits, for centuries, dwellers of Kashmir were expelled in the same manner from Kashmir, a nucleus, around which the Indian civilization spread in parts of India, China and West Asia, and which is a part of India like other federating states. Under the leadership of Mahmood of Ghazni on the western borders of India and later under Mohammed Ghouri, the Muslim tribes combined to try their luck in loot and subjugation of the Hindus. Throughout the thirteenth century they repeatedly entered India and after victory over Prithvi Raj Chauhan who had earlier thwarted Ghauri's raids on India, Delhi was secured as a centre for further raids and the expansion of the Delhi Islamic state. In the beginning of the 14th century Amir Taimur raided India but was surprised that Delhi was ruled by Muslims and he could not in conscience loot the residents, the subjects of a Muslim ruler. Still he got an excuse to loot Delhi to his heart's content. When he left Delhi in 1398 A.D. after a stay for less than a month in Delhi, his loot was carted away on fifty elephants.

Towards the close of the 15th century, Babar, a descendant of Amir Taimur started his invasions of India and set up Mughal rule at Delhi. His son Humayun was expelled from India by the despoiled Afghans under the leadership of Sher Shah Suri who had his power centre in Bihar. Though the Delhi state owed no allegiance to the Afghan or Iranian rule, yet as fellow Muslims they counted on these countries to provide them assistance against the Indians obstructing Islamic advance. Humayun sought assistance from Iran and was promptly given sufficient help so that he could raise a large army and also equip it. Humayun retook Delhi from Hemu, a Hindu self-appointed ruler of Delhi after he had worsted all Delhi commanders one by one and deposed the Lodhi ruler. Hemu is a very tragic figure in India's history.

Victory slipped from his hand on the field of battle when a chance arrow pierced his eye and killed him. Humayun's son and heir Akbar assumed the title of Emperor of Hindustan in 1526 and by his skill and personal ability especially to woo the Rajputs into an alliance for Mughal-*cum*-Rajput supremacy in India.

Akbar believed that the power of the state rested with the subjects and made all efforts to give a rule of justice for all subjects, Muslim or non-Muslim. Akbar was a secular person and respected all religions and their modes of worship. He even tried to found a new syncretic religion, Din-e-Illahi, inviting Muslims and non-Muslims to join without any conversion rites. He could hold his own in debates with preachers and priests of all religions like Hindu–Buddhism, Islam, Judaism or Christianity. He made all efforts to win the love of his subjects giving them rule of law and natural justice. His court was studded with brilliant men who had reached the summit in their calling.

Hindus and Muslims had fought to a stand-off and now were busy building a composite culture. Indians were more than ever confirmed in their belief in peaceful coexistence and ethical and secular values so necessary for civilized living. Throughout the so called Muslim period of Indian History (1200 A.D. to 1857A.D.) powerful Hindu kingdoms continued to prosper all over India like many Rajput states, Hindu kingdoms in Punjab, Himachal, Uttarakhand, Assam, Orissa, Vijaynagar empire, remnants of earlier Huns and Sakas who had adopted Hindu way of life in Malwa, many free tribes in the forest areas of central India, and coastal India, as in princely India under the British overlordship of the country. In fact the British control of princely India was much more compared to the relatively easy relations of independent states during the Muslim period requiring only an annual present to the Delhi emperor. Such loose control of the central power was its undoing, when Aurangzeb, the great grandson of Akbar usurped the throne at Delhi from the legitimate heir, his eldest brother, Dara Shikoh, a scholar of Sanskrit and raised to be a popular king of his subjects, both Hindu and Muslim, Aurangzeb was egged on towards rebellion by fanatic Muslim faction of the armed forces. Aurangzeb's actions like reimposition of Jazia a tax on non-Muslims and allowing the rule of Koranic injunctions to be enforced by religious courts of Muslim Kazis were offensive to his Hindu subjects.

Reacting to fanatical pursuit of an Islamic state in the whole of India, Aurangzeb hastened its break up and a Hindu rebellion, especially the uprising of the Sikhs in the Punjab, and the Marathas in Maharashtra. Another factor was the entry of European trading companies who got imperial permission to set up trading posts in India and soon had their own armed soldiers for guarding their property. With these forces they also entered Indian politics and expanded their possessions by alliances and counter alliances.

Most other trading companies were marginalized, but the British East India Company prospered through the skill of its officials in India and their pursuit of success by hook or by crook, it succeeded in controlling Bengal and soon were successful against the Marathas to control the emperor at Delhi as their pensioner. When the emperor became the appointed leader of the sepoys in their mutiny in 1857, he was deposed and exiled to Rangoon, and the English Queen became the empress of India.

2 Struggle for Freedom

2.1 Renaissance and National Consciousness

The ancient Indian texts and the history of the revolutionary movements in England were the eye openers for the Indians. On their arrival, the Britishers learnt of the past great achievements of Indian philosophers, astronomers and technicians. But they also realized the depths of despair when they looked at the burden of superstitions and social fissures in the Indian society. The reality of English literature and common sense in inter-relationships promoted renaissance in Indian thought and arts, especially in Bengal where the change agents were most active. The cream of Bengal society set up study circles for learning about Europe and the thrust of European nationalism and capitalism. The young men with the support of enlightened elders became active in contributing their beliefs and rebellious criticism of the follies that masqueraded as religion in India. The differential justice in company courts for Europeans and Indians opened their eyes to the caste structure of Indians including the casteless untouchables. They could see clearly the miserable position to which women in India were pushed down. The glaring faults of *sati* as well as child marriages were corroding the Indian society. The renaissance is best seen in the novels of Bankim Chandra Chatterjee and essays of Ishwar Chandra Vidyasagar. A thousand years of destruction of Hindu art and mutilation of Indian masterpieces of sculptures and temple idols and the loss of court patronage had brought Indian creative work almost to a standstill especially in north India.

The crippling of Indian industry was manipulated by control of imports and exports, whereas earlier India was attracting large amounts in gold and silver for its exports, it was now reduced to imports from England almost of everything from needles to road rollers. It was part of a new awakening that Indians realized the harm that was done to this country as a nation. A wave of *swadeshi, i.e.* preference to buy things that were made in India surged. It was an awakened Bengal that first tried the tactic of boycott of imports and attempted to start various industries and enterprises in Kolkata. The intelligentsia also persisted in their pride for the high reaches of Indian philosophy and traditional technology. A press was started. The Indian newspapers and magazines played a vigorous role in the renaissance of literature and poetry as well as reformist activity. Humanism and secularism were foremost in the Bengal mind at that time.

2.2 Seeds of Disunity

The British partitioned Bengal to reduce the spreading influence of reformist and revolutionary youth in rural East Bengal. This led to a mass movement in India and forced the British government to annul the partition. The British started recognizing India as a nation as long as it stayed a colony. They also sowed the seeds of disunity by conferring special representation on Muslims and other minorities, colonial style, in a so called democracy extended to British India. Their nefarious policy succeeded beyond their own expectations. They partitioned India, as a result of which Bengal and Punjab were partitioned.

An English daily *Bande Matram* was started in 1906 propagating rebellion and freedom from foreign bondage. In 1878 A.D. there were 478 newspapers in the Company-controlled territories. The writings of Deenbandhu, Naved Chandra Sen, B.C. Chatterjee among others were soul stirring. The period 1875-1884 has been dubbed the seed time of Indian independence. In 1885, the Indian National Congress was formed. The moderates among the Indian leadership believed in the continuation of the British rule as they sincerely felt that they were the best change agents and educators needed in India.

The government was primarily interested in transferring wealth to England on every excuse. They did not work in the interest of the Indian nation or the Indians. They had no policy to fight frequent famines or the shortage of food or water in various parts of the country. It was certainly not a state working in the interest of India. In 1914 there was a big challenge to the British, when the First Great War (1914-1918) began. India including the Indian National Congress, wanted to fight alongside the British, but objected that the latter should not have unilaterally declared India to be at war on the side of the Anglo-French alliance. The British authorities gave declarations that when the war was over they were going to increase Indian democratic participation in running their affairs. Major famines visited company territories in 1837, 1875 and also later. To the utter consternation of Indians, the British attempted to tighten their grip on the country. They empowered the judges to try political cases without juries and the provincial governors were given the power of internment. Both Mahatma Gandhi and Bal Gangadhar Tilak condemned this in the strongest terms. Then occurred in 1919, the Jallianwala Bagh tragedy when a peaceful protest meeting in Amritsr was gunned down by the orders of a British general without regard to the safe exit of the people, who were entrapped at the site. The atrocities were the last straw for the Indian forbearance and they became all set to carry on the struggle for total independence.

2.3 Diarchy

In diarchy dispensation, all important departments of government were controlled by the British viceroy and the British home office in London. The years 1919 to 1929 were the years of diarchy when the Montagu-Chelmsford reforms were put into effect in the

Government of India Act of 1919. In the central legislature, the Swarajya Party, a faction of the Congress agreed to work as required in the reforms, while the Congress boycotted the diarchy governments of the provinces. In the Punjab and Madras, reforms came up to the expectations of the British. The British government invited Indian leaders to a Round Table Conference in London to hammer out a suitable new Act to replace the Act of 1919. Mahatma Gandhi was the sole Congress representative to attend the same. The Congress expected the Muslim League represented by Mohammed Ali Jinnah to be loyal to the national cause in view of the Lucknow Pact between the League and the Congress with the Congress having accepted certain weightage to Muslims in the legislature, though it was against the principle of universal suffrage and secular joint electorate. Mr. Jinnah showed no flexibility. The British had another card to play that the depressed classes of the Hindus represented by Dr. Ambedkar should have separate electorate from the Hindus and the Muslims. Here Mahatma Gandhi staked his life in a hunger strike against that measure as it would perpetuate untouchability. There was widespread movement in India supporting Mahatma Gandhi and soon untouchability was abolished by law in India. The Mahatma's life was saved and the proposal to split the non-Muslim electorate was dropped.

2.4 Provincial Autonomy

The Government of India Act enacted in 1935 was a device for perpetuating control of the British but was couched in phrases conveying the intention to develop India's ability for self-rule. It created diarchy (which had already failed in the provinces) now to be tried at the centre. It confirmed the communal award and attempted to wean away the religious minorities from the national struggle for independence. Soon some Muslim leaders started claiming that India was inhabited by two nations : Hindu and Muslim and even drew maps indicating the establishment of

Pakistan as the homeland of Indian Muslims. When eventually Pakistan was established it was dubbed by Jinnah as moth-eaten Pakistan as no corridor was allotted across Hindu India for connecting the two wings of Pakistan ! Today there are more Muslims living in India than in Pakistan, but the two nation theory of the All India Muslim League is taking hard time to lay buried. The terrorist organizations spawned outside India are funding the hard to spot Indian Muslim students or others for their nefarious ends. The training camps are operating in Pakistan and fringe territories owing allegiance to Osama Bin Laden, the supremo of the Al Qaeda Jihadi outfit aiming at prying out the J&K state from the Indian Union since it has Muslim majority and according to them was wrongly prevailed upon to join India. This Muslim majority state had voluntarily joined India, a secular state, since the Muslim tribes in the west of the state along with Pakistan army unleashed a lethal attack on the helpless people of Kashmir especially the non-Muslims.

The elections under separate electoral system were held and the Indian National Congress came in majority in most of the British Indian provinces including two of the Muslim majority provinces of Sind and NWFP also part of the sketch map of Pakistan as proposed by the Muslim League in their propaganda. The Congress ministries resigned in protest in 1939 when the British Secretary of State for India who was the colonial puppet master unilaterally declared India to be at war with the axis powers. The Muslim League celebrated the occasion as a deliverance day. Mahatma Gandhi had authorized individual Satyagraha against the violence let loose in the world. The Government of India tried to suppress the movement. In 1941, Hitler attacked the Soviet Union. According to the Communist Party of India the war changed from an imperialist war to a people's war and offered all out help to the British unconditionally. The Communist Party was then allowed by them to function freely. The main job, the party undertook was to now argue for the two-nation theory and to collaborate with the Muslim League in its aim of partition of India.

2.5 Freedom and Partition

Finding the world situation getting critical for democracy and regarding the inaction by the nationalists in India as time wasted, the Congress passed the Quit India Resolution on August 9,1942. Mahatma Gandhi gave the clarion call to "Do or Die". The entire Congress leadership was imprisoned. Still the leaderless workers rebelled and for a few weeks, the entire government administration was expelled from Bihar and Bengal. Many dormant rebellious movements activated themselves among the Sikhs and the Muslims.

An indirect result was the inner confidence achieved by Netaji, a former President of the Congress who had attracted Indian diaspora in East Asia and the Indian prisoners of war in the Japanese prison camps to fight for India's freedom from outside India. The INA (Indian National Army) was recognized by the Japanese for its national struggle against the British. Netaji Subhas Chandra Bose's army attacked British Indian troops from their bases in Burma (Myanmar) and the Andamans which were handed over to them by the Japanese forces. When the war ended in 1945, a big change had occurred in the expectations of India in spite of no progress towards more self-government. Various proposals emanating from London like the offers by Stafford Cripps tried to salvage the unity of India. There had been a phenomenal unity managed by Netaji who raised a liberation army composed of released prisoners of war in Japanese control, and successfully attacked across Indian eastern borders reaching up to Kohima. His heroic deeds galvanized revolts in the Indian Air Force and the Indian Navy. This hastened the Labour government's resolve in London to fix the date of relinquishing power in India. The Secretary of State for India in London announced that the British would relinquish power in India by the 14th August, 1947 and in the absence of unity, hand over government to the Muslim leaders in Karachi and the Congress leaders in Delhi on the 15th August

1947 after partitioning the country into India and Pakistan composed of an eastern wing and a western wing. The Radcliff award regarding the partition of certain states would be announced before independence. Both Nehru and Jinnah believed that after the acceptance of the Pakistan demand by the British and the Indian leaders, both parts of India temporarily as British dominions, will provide peaceful home to the minorities that decided to stay in each dominion. They, however did not, gauge the depths to which the Muslim mobs had been indoctrinated against the non-Muslims who might stay on in Pakistan. Immediately on seeing the certainty of Muslim rule in Pakistan, the Muslim League zealots with the connivance of the police started pogroms against the non-Muslims in NWFP, Sind and the Punjab. Immediately as a reaction, anti-Muslim pogroms in spite of opposition from the police, were unleashed in Bihar and in pockets around Delhi and some western districts of East Punjab. The sad story of partition riots can never be fully written; about a million people were killed and about ten million people migrated from both dominions seeking refuge in the other dominion. Refugees kept on reaching their destinations for a few months after independence and the two new governments started joint operations for the safety of the refugees on the march and for escort of isolated cases trapped unwillingly in the wrong dominion. Mahatma Gandhi saw to it that there was repatriation of share of state assets fairly to Pakistan from India.

2.6 Integration of India

When Pakistan made a violent effort to grab the J&K state by unleashing a tribal attack, the Maharaja of the state was jolted to seek aid from India to repel the attack, and as a necessary condition, he signed the document of accession of the state. India dispatched sufficient force to Srinagar in order to repel the attack of the tribal militia and also complained to the UN for restraining Pakistan. Pakistan waged another unsuccessful war in 1965 for their aim of annexation of J&K state camouflaging it as a war for liberating that state. India later annexed the French territories within India peacefully and the Portuguese pockets with some show of force. Goa now has the status of a federating state of India. This was done along with getting the Nizam of Hyderabad to sign the document of accession to India. The Junagarh Nawab had to be expelled when he delayed merging his tiny state into India as desired by his subjects. Similarly the tiny kingdom of Sikkim had to give up dreams of sovereignty by playing on the differences of Tibet with China. The only shortcoming in the territorial integrity of India is the portion of the J&K state that Pakistan gifted to China since India had not yet extended its defensive positions there. The matter will be sorted out when India and China reach their border agreement. India has extended its administration to the eastern borders with Myanmar. Many autonomous North East Indian states have been created federating in principle in the Indian Union. There are some pending differences about the sharing of the wealth of the region after development, about the ambition of the Nagaland state to extend its boundaries to include different clans of Nagas living peacefully in other North East Indian states. India cannot allow such a destabilizing ambition of a state. Any redrawing of borders of states is to be left to the democratic popular will.

We have touched on the integration of some problem states within the Indian Union. There were hundreds of other princely states— some as large as Mysore and Jaipur and some as small as Kashi—all these peacefully integrated into the Union of India through the humane handling of Nehru and the skill of Sardar Patel, the first Home Minister of free India. A sad consequence of partition of India was that a misguided young Hindu shot and killed Gandhi holding him responsible for the surrender of the Congress to the outrageous Muslim demand for the partition of India. The fact is that Gandhi was the lone voice opposed to acceptance of partition by the Congress. The acceptance of partition by the Congress leadership had become necessary after the failure of the joint effort of the Congress with the Muslim League to run the country in 1946. The cancer of Hindu-Muslim divide had bitten deep into the middle classes in most parts of India. It is this upsurge of desire to live in a free Muslim homeland that moved most of the Muslim civil servants in U.P., Punjab, Central Province and Bombay Presidency etc. to migrate to Pakistan after independence. The Muslim masses in India preferred to stay put unless forced to flee by local rioting. Most of the rioting took place in Pakistan when the power was still with the British civil and military officers in India, who had always held that given a chance, the Hindus and Muslims will be flying at each others' throats. This actually happened only in the Muslim League majority areas and retaliation was made by new forces of Hindu chauvinism unleashed by League's uncompromising attitude. These new forces also conspired to murder Gandhi, the architect of Indian freedom.

2.7 Christians in India

Christians of India, in popular view, were the creation of the British Indian government for getting a set of people most impressed with the British hold on India and so was the case for the Anglo Indians. The Constituent Assembly demanded by the Indians and set up in agreement with the departing British authority prepared a constitution that is a marvel of mature political thought and understanding of the requirements of India as a free country. Complete liberty to pursue one's religion without giving offence to neighbours was enshrined in the Constitution. Provision of nomination of additional representation in the legislative bodies was made to ensure the presence of accredited spokesmen of the microscopic minorities in the Parliament. In spite of liberal availability for migration to UK or to Australia, practically all Anglo-Indians stayed on in India and prospered by their ability and industry. Some depressed classes converted to Christianity were welcome in Pakistan initially, but most of them returned later to India because they found the unlisted bias against the depressed classes too strong there while in India amelioration of the status of the depressed classes was continuous and dramatic.

2.8 India—A Sovereign Republic

India declared itself a republic on January 26, 1950 choosing the day in memory of the complete independence resolution passed on that day by the All India Congress annual session at Lahore in 1929 under the presidentship of Jawaharlal Nehru.

India had now the tradition of celebrating the Republic Day by holding a military marchpast in Delhi along with cultural tableaux. Similar events are held in all state capitals. At Delhi, the salute is taken by the President of India. It is customary to invite some foreign head of state to be the chief guest on the occasion. The Delhi parade also displays any civil or military new hardware produced in the past year.

3 Democracy in India

3.1 Organization Development

For a nation to progress, it must be involved in decision-making. The best form of governance for this purpose is democracy. In a democracy, rules, laws and decisions are made by the people. Democracy is a form of organization and functioning. Every citizen has an equal voice in the election of the representatives. This is termed universal adult suffrage. The entire electorate is divided into a number of constituencies and each one of these elects by secret ballot a specified number of legislators. The legislators of the majority or coalition choose a Prime Minister who then selects a team of colleagues who individually and collectively are responsible to the legislature, but hold office only at the pleasure of the President, who is advised by the Prime Minister. In principle, a simple majority of legislators runs the government but in actual working, every measure must have majority support which is only possible if the popular support is first enlisted by discussions and the committee work and views of others are assimilated before a measure in final form is drafted. Democracy is not dictatorship of the majority. The power has to be exercised in the interest of the poor and specifically of the poorest according to the philosophy of Mahatma Gandhi. Gaddafi type true democracy can be possible only in a small population when the citizens themselves vote in a public referendum. The Panchayat system prevailing in Indian villages from ancient times is based on direct democracy. Democracy in India is somewhat patterned on the British parliamentary system. Governing a country like India in the interest of the Indian people and keeping in mind the imperatives of external and internal security is a tremendous task. The essentials of an election commission and an independent judiciary are in place. An active judiciary is engaged in goading the local bodies and public services to adopt transparent policies and provide time bound services to the people. Redressal of public complaints is attempted through simplified judicial procedures.

Legalistic procrastination is slowing down the dispensation of justice. The government could appoint judges for life (or till they ask to be relieved). The age on recruitment could be raised to 32 years for candidates with post-graduate qualification in some basic science, social science or management. Judges need not be identified in any way with the legal profession.

The mixed economy including a vibrant public sector for initiating new industries based on new technologies or by investing public funds in research and development work for technological advances, which is the only way for competitive position in production and new commercial lines. Rural credit has to be multiplied to utilize the mass creativity lying dormant in villages. First consideration must be the provision of remunerative work and employment and old age pension for all especially the women folk. Recently introduced central schemes for rural health, rural housing and rural employment are popular with the masses. Cooperative production with other like-minded countries can be explored for making headway in the development and production of new products at present monopolized by developed countries like power generation equipment, armament as trade items, space exploitation and plums ensuing from bio-technology and nano-technology.

For an effective popular government, it should have a convincing majority in Parliament. The centrist Congress did form a coalition government with the outside support of the Communists. The stage is now of united action both for the nation as well as for the world. The Congress could now hope to form a national front with the Communists and prevail upon them to join and support the common policies from inside the government. Congress would do well to go for fresh elections if necessary on the basis of formation of a national government with the Gandhi and Nehru inspired basic policies of all-round development and soft corner for the long range prosperity of the underprivileged. This calls for a continuous effort and nurturing by hard work and creativity.

3.2 Subversion of Democracy

Historically, kingship has flourished all over the world. India thrived on village democracy but preferred kings to rule over larger areas by public acceptance or through expansion by military conquests. Popular conception of the king was a father figure demanding respect and obedience. Even after Independence of India and elimination of princes who were truly lords of all that was existing in their petty kingdoms, a general in the Indian army would show in many ways his respect and devotion to the petty prince of his home state. In princely India there were no elections and no democracy. The kings and princes lived in a feudal world using the resources of their principalities primarily for themselves or their feudal followers and religious bigwigs who always supported the rulers. The imperial overlords duly collected their share. Kings and parliaments rarely mix. Parliamentary democracy along with a ceremonial kingship survived only in U.K. after long drawn out strife. Parliamentary rule with an elected president for a limited term is now the norm for most countries. Most people realize the value of parliamentary system for the transition from one set of rulers to the next. The parliamentary system can also be thwarted from providing a truly democratic government; there could be rigged elections, physical interruption of voters to cast their votes if they are likely to cast adverse votes etc. A simpler device is to cultivate self-appointed leaders of recognized vote banks of dumb driven voters swayed by slogans of religion, community or livelihood to be in danger. Only now after many decades have the Indian voters shaken off the hold of illiterate religious priests or frog in the well scholars. False alarms of danger to national security or to private property and private savings is another device to sway the public to vote for demagogues and reactionary "revolutionaries". The parliamentary voting system is often subverted by money power and can be countered only by active media drumming for sensible scientific approach and diligently spreading the new horizons being opened by science and technology and exposing every kind of humbug being thrust on the innocent voter.

A constant danger to any system of government is from corruption and self aggrandizement by people entrusted to execute the policies, *i.e.* the bureaucracy. Bureaucracy is very necessary for appointing contractors, for releasing funds, supervising and auditing as well as carrying out sundry functions. Simple notices in public places that all attempts at illegal gratification should be reported to the vigilance officer whose contact address or phone number is duly displayed, will not curb corruption. This only provides an alibi to the official sitting behind the notice to ask and receive illegal gratification for himself and his colleagues and superiors. An ordinary police station is engaged in lucrative estate management of all side-walk business sites, all legitimate goods carrying traffic. The police must be turning a blind eye to criminal activities of various kinds if regular protection premiums were paid. The only way to combat corruption is an up-to-date inspection and auditing of the work output, by capable and honest highly paid auditing officials. An official when seen to be corrupt must be shifted from the seat and suitably punished. Only one appeal to the higher authorities may be considered admissible.

Many inept bureaucrats will hide behind inaction and inefficiency. This only causes double damage to the government. The public opens channels of corruption to get their work done in time for their requirements and the inefficiency of one official begets inefficiency elsewhere in the administration. Inefficiency is a prelude to corrupt practices. In the transparent mode of conducting work, inefficiency is reduced without harming the accountability of all concerned. The office routine should be simple and the flow of information rapid without needless involvement of irrelevant signatures of senior officials. The aims and philosophy of working must be clear and acceptable to all cogs in the machine so that there is smooth and constructive work at all quarters. The commitment of the bureaucracy must be honesty and clear expression as well to the success of the official policies and views.

Subversion of democracy occurs when the voters are not intelligently involved in the choices before the nation and the legislators depend only on populist measures ignoring the reality of economics and limitations of trained and capable staff. If national efforts for production and expansion of skills of the populace are being neglected with most energy going into celebrations and strikes and reliance on the rhetoric of demagogues and rabble rousers, there is bound to be rude awakening when silently revolution brews and there is sudden burst of anger and disorder. A two-party system is an insurance against any violent shakeup. Every legislation has to be carefully drafted to include the needs of the whole population. In India, at start, the voters were with the national leaders, who had worked and suffered during the struggle for independence. These acceptable leaders sought to achieve their continuance in the saddle by resorting to vote bank politics, by seeking support of illiterate religious bigwigs and money and muscle power often of questionable means. There was a backlash and chauvinistic elements of religion and fascist tendency among capitalists created countrywide following for pursuit of ancient glory of fact and myth. The constructive majority of the population was elbowed out and the country had a taste of wild goose chase of power without any true sense of world affairs or of the powerful choices springing from science and technology. The new means of mass communication marginalized much of the pull of ignorant priests and traditional rituals. In India there is now a move to have a code of personal law which will cater to the needs of all groups and there is common sense approach to future changes in matrimonial regulations and inheritance laws. One can expect thorough revision for the good in these matters in the next couple of decades through discussions and conferences. In spite of large numbers involved, the Dalits (depressed classes), the tribals and women could never muster enough support in the legislature for speedy attention to their problems and empowerment. By sheer goodwill of the majority, these neglected sectors are now in the limelight and many rules are being framed to grant them more say in the affairs of the country and especially in matters concerning them without reference to their religious, state or caste affiliation. The fruits of freedom and globalization must reach all people. Dictatorship of the majority, of the proletariat or of capital or the ulema (scholarly custodians of tradition) is totally repudiated in a true democracy.

Management by discussion, consensus, with boldness in execution and with the spirit of sacrifice from the beneficiaries, are essential for all-round progress. This stage has been reached by India.

3.3 World Governance

The world is still constituted of independent nations who are finding many common concerns. A nation's progress and progress of other nations is no longer a zero sum game. A nation progresses now in tune with neighbouring as well as distant nations. The stresses imposed by rapid progress should not mean a reason to be jealous, mean or proud. Like an individual, nations have so many reasons to be obliged for friendly assistance to many countries. The coming together of independent nations in the UN is a remarkable post-war development. The UN reflects human aspirations for peace and cooperation. The UN promotes ideals of total disarmament, control of atomic energy, space and the seas in the interest of the whole world. UN is entrusted with many aspects of world governance. The International Court of Justice at the Hague often deals with formal structure of international law and its observance. The UN governance is through international conferences and recommendations to be voluntarily adopted by various nations. The Security Council is often made ineffective through the veto allowed to victors of the last war. The UN is likely to become more democratic and have a larger Security Council and the veto power as an ultimate insurance against irreparable damage to some nations held guilty, the veto will be exercised by a more acceptable peace council yet to be introduced. Certain tasks carried out by the UN like fight against narcotics trade, piracy, supervision of truce after conflict, patrolling of international frontiers and to provide confidence to any threatened nation, require police powers and military contingents. So far voluntary assignment of military contingents from national armed forces for UN duties is resorted to. Still some permanent police force directly seconded to the UN might be of benefit. This force will coordinate all UN police actions and planning and have a core body of leading experts for the supervision of national programmes aiming at disarmament and control of weapons and the arms trade. For all this the UN could be assigned certain funds as national contributions as well as certain taxes and business profits. A UN tax may be levied on all international travel. Certain cities and heritage sites may be declared as sites of peace requiring no visas for entry and exit by UN sponsored means of travel. Such sites will be administered by UN civil authority and allowed certain productive and gainful enterprises for the UN like education and training for business exploitation of world greens like the deep seas, high mountains, frozen wilds, artificial island platforms and management of special tasks in exploration, space travel and astronomy. The UN should have the power to recommend special measures to concerned national governments for the peaceful development of neglected segments of people especially striding the borders of different countries. A system of UN controlled armament depots will look after the surplus armaments of nations and their eventual safe destruction. A UN tax will be levied on nuclear power as well as wind and solar power for civil use. UN taxes will be collected by national governments and transferred to UN run banks. A UN sponsored insurance company will sell insurance against terrorism, epidemics and pollution based damage. Thus in a steady and controlled fashion an international world governance will come into being. A UN publication programme will expand in promoting science and technology for worldwide reconstruction effort including modernization of religious beliefs which have to co-exist with continuing scientific advances. Certain national media and television channels will be associated with UN sponsored " whole world—one family" programmes.

3.4 Secularism

Secular democracy emphasizes the equality of democratic rights irrespective of caste, creed or religious label. Democracy in India loaded by the colonial regime with communal electorates has been disruptive of the Indian society and its slow and steady integration. The present democracy includes traditional secularism, *i.e.* the right to be free from education mixed with religious dogma of any kind. Outside India, secularism is often taken to be atheism and denial of religious practices and observances, not so in India. Nehru defined Indian secularism to mean equal respect to all religions. In case, observing the traditional practice of one's religion is offensive to followers of another religion, Indian culture and secularism allow one to ignore the traditional practice and to modify one's practice of religion to adopt an acceptable style. In the secular approach, according to the Secular Life Society of India, a secular person will have social and business relations with others purely on merits and not on considerations of caste, creed or religion. India has been declared a secular state, *i.e.* it shows no partiality to any particular religion. Colonial government in principle was also secular in this sense, but it was indifferent to the content of religion. Free India is not indifferent to reform in all religions and the need for simultaneous admission of scientific facts and human achievements in the spiritual realm. The nation looks down on actions which indicate sacrilege of structure and symbols sacred to some religion or the other. According to Nehru, new temples of India are the scientific laboratories where human beings wrestle with ignorance. The Americans are proud of Israel's internal democracy, but that state has been built on violent suppression of a large population in the former Palestine. Only peaceful coexistence and brotherly relations between new Palestine and more developed Israel will bring about peace in West Asia, then the power of Islamic terrorists will begin to crumble.

Indian traditional culture is humanist and secular. The secularist India and fanatical faction of Muslims have been struggling for the mind of Kashmiri Muslims and indications are that fanaticism has lost. Even within Pakistan voices of reason are recalling the traditional fellowship that was developing between Muslims and non-Muslims. Kashmiri Muslims have also inherited the views of the Muslim poets and *rishis* of Kashmir. *Rishi* is the title of the ancient Hindu thinkers and scholars who composed the *Vedas* and other scriptures of the Hindus. With the advent of Islam in Kashmir, there was fellowship between the Hindu *rishis* and the Muslim divines who also came to be known as *rishis*. The *rishis* on both sides exhorted people to live in fellowship. When in the sixteenth century, fanatical Dards, a Muslim tribe of western Kashmir sought to overrun Kashmir, the population of Kashmir sought merger into Mughal India and since then Kashmir has been a part of political India while it had a leadership role in the Hindu-Buddhist tradition of humanism and secularism.

3.5 Religious Conversion

Secular approach includes freedom to practice any religion. If the essence of religion is faith and a particular philosophy of life, there should be freedom to discuss and debate. In India religious debates were quite common like the TV debates in electioneering in USA. The debate was settled by the clamour of the audience since the debates were held in the open. People took to new philosophies, but there was never a demand for religious conversion. It is on this account that within Indian religions there is a multitude of beliefs. Since there was a form of coexistence of various religions, the need of religious conversion was missing. The social life of most people was in traditional religious celebrations of all kinds. Religious conversion started being a problem when colonial type democracy went by numbers sporting different religious labels. The conversion to Christianity of Karens in Burma (Myanmar) showed the denationalizing influence of conversion when Karens refused to welcome freedom of Burma. Secular India allows conversion freely chosen by the possible convert, but if there is a sign of extraneous considerations, the society does not favour conversion. In India inter-religious marriages now take place and can be solemnized without one party being forced to convert to the religion of the other party. In Indonesia, conversion to Islam did not mean giving up also of usual names originating in Sanskrit for names in Arab or Persian style. A convert is usually estranged from the companionship provided by participation in traditional festivals and processions. Indonesian Muslims continued with ancient culture of dances and music and the nation experienced stability. The conversion in India after the political emphasis on religious distinction has meant that the convert should uproot himself from most aspects of village life. This has meant denationalization and is, therefore, frowned upon.

3.6 Women

Women in India were first idealized, then idolized, and then enslaved. Women's role as mother and in bringing up children was given all consideration. Indian history is full of mothers who were tutors of their children who rose to become kings and emperors. Idolization of women is apparent in widespread worship of goddesses. The consorts of god-heroes have precedence as in the chants, Sita-Ram or Radhe-Shyam. Hindus did not bind the feet of their women like the Chinese, nor did they put them behind the veil. They, however, were declared unfit to be taught the *Vedas* and the *Shastras*. In the middle ages, they were denied education beyond the 3 R's. Discrimination against women in public life was torn to shreds only when they started participating shoulder to shoulder in the freedom struggle in the twentieth century. Today India has women prospering in every field of activity. An Indian woman was the President of the UN General Assembly. Christian missions were the pioneers in modern education of women. Indian reformers after close contact with Europeans in Bengal were active in promoting gender equality. A bill has been introduced to ensure at least thirty per cent representation in the Indian Parliament for women. India is hoping for reform in their marriage and inheritance laws and seeks to enact a common civil code through consensus building.

Women employment in the organized sector is very low, only 4 per cent. Women sometimes are engaged to work in highly hazardous working conditions with little social security to back them. Since independence women have occupied small number of seats in Lok Sabha. Women are now being elected to local councils in large numbers. India has ratified the UN convention for elimination of all forms of discrimination against women. Women in India are now joining the army and the police force. Women in India particularly in urban areas are quite aware of the new opportunities that are available. Inheritance laws have to be reframed along with socially desirable dowry practices. The empowerment of women involves economic opportunity and personal rights. Swami Vivekananda said "there is no chance for the welfare of a society unless the condition of the women improves." In public sector women constituted 13.8 per cent of the total workforce in 1997 and 13.9 per cent women were employed in government. In 2001 there were 31.3 per cent women in Panchayati Raj. Female literacy rate rose to 54 per cent in 2001 and has been rising. Women carry out some regular chores in the family which are not registered anywhere for remuneration. India, as a welfare measure, has decided to give women old age pension recognizing their life long work for their families. This suggestion was first given by the senior author in his version of a measure of welfare economics. Rural women involved in agriculture constitute 78 per cent of the economically active population of women in India. Women are poorly represented in our political parties and in the state and national legislatures. The political parties are now endeavouring to nominate more women to contest elections in future. In 1999, there were 48 women members of parliament compared to 22 in 1951. The National Commission for Women is quite active in promoting women NGOs spreading information and knowledge of their rights and giving them assistance in benefiting from many state schemes regarding education and training. For the first time India has elected a woman to be the President of the Republic.

3.7 Depressed Classes

Depressed classes of India have suffered discrimination of various kinds including untouchability from middle ages. The origin is lost in some misdeeds of some ancient ancestor who got excommunicated in his village by unanimous vote in the village Panchayat. On account of isolation of villages, when the excommunication stuck to him and his family, it would drive him to engage in some unclean work and then the family and descendants would also be available for unclean work as outcastes who became untouchables to various degrees. The requirement for able labour for unclean professions was so great that punishing certain class of sins and crimes by declaring the family outcaste spread. The proportion of outcastes and untouchables grew to about 20 per cent. It was only the threatened separate communal vote for them that hastened the reformist action, that had grown since the spread of the Bhakti movement and the zeal of the Arya Samaj and of Mahatma Gandhi, for the suppression of untouchability which was like a form of slavery when the untouchables worked only for tips and not wages. New communication and mobility helped them escape social tyranny. Now such discrimination is illegal. The untouchables without schooling or financial resources were extremely poor and even after economic well-being of the country, the lot of the depressed classes was dismal. The colonial government had dubbed many tribals as belonging to criminal tribes. Independent India under the inspiration of Jawaharlal Nehru made efforts first to allow the primitive jungle folk to stay in safe isolation and develop according to their own customs and tribal wisdom. This did not help them much and they continued to live under tutelage of their illiterate and unskilled elders. India is now endeavouring to vest them with property rights on the minor jungle produce and to promote settled life in villages in their own habitat. They are being provided with facilities of education and funds for cooperative selling of herbs and cures. If the depressed classes learn to use their voting strength to their own advantage, the main line political parties would be trying their best to induce them to promote their nominees in elections. In one Indian state, already the Dalits have formed the government. Their political parties now are exerting to form coalition governments at the centre and in many states. Many learned men and women from all walks of life and of all castes and religions are sympathetic to their cause. Dalit literature has made a niche for itself in Indian literature particularly in Marathi and Hindi. A private Ramnika Foundation run by an upper caste Punjabi poetess and a patriotic communist, is supporting Dalit literature and their national magazines. Dr. Ambedkar, their most prominent leader, who joined Gandhi to demolish the colonial conspiracy to separate Dalit vote from the rest of the Hindu voting strength, advised the Dalits to become Buddhists and escape feudal trap of servitude to the upper caste Hindus. Many Dalits have followed Ambedkar's advice and raised him to the coveted status of a Bodhisattva whose idols can be worshipped. Caste Hindus are not unhappy on this conversion since they themselves revere the Buddha as an incarnation of

Vishnu and freely worship in Buddhist temples. The national government and the main line political parties are very much conscious of the guilt carried by the nation for the mistreatment of depressed classes. They are keen to make amends within reason. They have made reservation of seats in institutions of advanced academic as well as professional learning and in government posts and are also trying to get some jobs reserved in private industry for depressed class candidates. Even promotion posts within an organization have a proportion reserved for depressed classes. Such suppression of merit based selection and promotion of appointees should continue only for a limited period say, for another ten years or so.

3.8 Coalition Partners

When people and press have all the freedom to discuss and advise, there is bound to be multiplicity of views. There is a multiplicity of political parties as well. Most Indians are partial to a foreign policy of peace and centrist policies of the Congress that led the peaceful fight for freedom. In such a system, a simple parliamentary system of two major parties is not stable but two major coalitions can come to exist as has happened in India. The time is almost ripe for a national coalition with pragmatic leaning on different philosophies with the primary aim of advance of national prosperity and gross national happiness. The next best would be two major coalitions contending with different priorities for detailed blueprints of advancement. The popular parties are the Congress (broadly following Nehru's policies of mixed economy, socialism and secularism) and BJP (claiming to be a nationalist and socialist party and advocating guiding the illiterate masses through familiar ancient Hindu drives). There is a well knit Communist Party of India with its war time siding with the colonial power and the two-nation theory trotted by the Muslim League, now almost forgotten. It, however, has a feud with CPI-Marxist who prefer Maoist rhetoric to parliamentary incarnation of the CPI. The CPI had decided to keep BJP led coalition out of power by supporting the Congress led coalition from outside on issue based support. The record of the Communists anywhere in the world shows that at the first opportunity if they calculate it to be in the interest of international communism they will make the situation precarious and force others to join them to form a national government on their terms. Recently, realism made the Congress led coalition government in India with outside support of the leftist parties stable. The Communists tried to force the government to follow their line against close relations with the USA regarding atomic energy and strategic planning. The Communists withdrew their outside support on the issue of India-US accord on civilian nuclear agreement. But the government survived as many other parties rallied to its support since India could ill afford to give up the option of serving the world through cooperation with the USA while seeking cooperation with all nations including Russia and China.

A mixed economy and balancing of central planning with district-wise planning is going to be the key to economic progress. All projects have to be managed through various steps of total planning including the initial value analysis, feasibility and scientific management. Project planning would start in time, but the credit for any part of the project must be claimed only on the completion of that part. Allotment of funds is not such a big deal, but the returns from the project in terms of money, goods or happiness are credit worthy. Only proper management can avoid cost and time overruns. The Indian non-alignment now stands for alignment for any plan with all like-minded nations. We believe in unfettered trade with USA and Russia, China and Japan, Israel and Middle Eastern countries, all African and South American countries, the Commonwealth countries and developed and other developing countries of Europe. Globalization for India means prosperity and remunerative work for all. Development is no longer a zero-sum game.

India and Pakistan are now expected to engage in pragmatic closing of the ranks to mutual advantage particularly in combating international terrorism.

4 India-Pakistan Distrust and Current Thaw

4.1 Let us Bury the Hatchet

In September 2006, there was a newspaper headline that India and Pakistan should resolve afresh to settle all their differences by mutual discussion including the problem of the J&K State of India to which Pakistan has been laying a claim. There were perhaps some compulsions that prevented Pakistan from responding to so many hints and gestures from India for re-establishment of peace between the two countries and peaceful resolution of problems as they arose. We are happy that those compulsions no longer hamper the progress of our two countries in peace and cooperation. We have to consciously step out of the atmosphere of fear and hatred generated by the partition riots and the political immaturity that forced wars between India and Pakistan or India and Pakistan's ally China. Another ally of Pakistan who was at one time almost ready to pull Pakistan's chestnuts out of the fire for them, is now wooing both Pakistan and India for the world's fight against terrorism and seems keen that India and Pakistan quit antagonism in the interest of world peace and progress especially of South Asian countries.

When Pakistan also follows Musharraf into ways of peace with India, it is the golden opportunity for Muslims there to listen to the true teachings of Islam, the religion of peace. They ought no longer to trust the so-called fundamentalists who spread hatred garbed as religion. All religions are based on love and fellowship.

One has to control the strength that comes from fellowship and pious living so that it is channelled into ways of peace and progress and not selfish despoiling of rights of others. All religious leaders whether Hindu, Buddhist, Christian, Muslim or Sikh bear this in mind. Apart from usual prayers, explicit prayer for more wisdom to love others as self must be introduced in all lands. It is about time that the political leaders in both countries analyse the reasons that have caused the apparently religious label based split of Muslims and non-Muslims of the same environment in India and Pakistan. It was the neglect of basic humanism of religion under the deluded self-interest of a third party, the colonial imperialism imposed on both the countries. Putting aside the well known humanism of the English literature and poetic genius, the British rulers of India introduced ill-conceived colonial compartmentalized democracy in India in the form of communal label electorates. It has been hard to dismantle this legacy even in India, the cradle of humanism in the world. Voices of communal and caste reservation in jobs are lingering and vested interests are busy extending the virus of division. All individuals have to advance both in this world as well as in the next world on their own efforts and merit as the Buddha taught. The society has to assure the spread of merit in all its activities. Violent suppression of non-conformists and total assurance in one's own beliefs are only symptoms of failure. The blood baths and cleansing of areas from minorities only leads to creating refugees and a taste for loot and crime. The separatism planted by the colonial government was coming into bloom. When ripe it resulted in a blood bath of giant proportions when millions of common Hindus and Muslims lost life or limb and became refugees.

In the mind of a Pakistani there was a continuity, from Alexander's victory over Porus or the extension of the Iranian empire to include a part of the present Pakistan by the 8th century to the hit and run raids of Ghaznavi on the temple cities of India in the 11th century. He even regarded the havoc wrought by Chengiz Khan and Halaku as Allah's punishment meted out to the Hindus, when they actually destroyed the Arab-Iranian combine lording over West Asia. He imagined that it was the natural order of things that West Asian Muslims proceeded further with the good work of idol breaking started by the Byzentines in West Asia. The peak of modern day iconoclastic zeal was displayed by the Taliban created by Pakistan in their Madrasas who destroyed the world wonder site of giant Buddha statues on the hills near Bamian in Afghanistan, while the entire world was sad who valued the art and the memory of the ancestors who erected those wonders before the fifth century A.D. The contemporary leaders of Pakistan have to contend with the average polluted mind of their citizens by allowing them full access to genuine democracy and educating them in modern advances in history, science and technology and true situation in the modern world that promises piety as well as plenty if only man will give up hate and jealousy. An apt example of hate and jealousy also is provided by Pakistan in its early years of independence. While India was contending with woes of partition aggravated by Pakistani flood of tribals to rapine and loot the Indian state of J & K, India was again hit by one of the recurring food shortages because of the long neglect of steps necessary to build up sufficient food reserves, and when the international community particularly the USA was considering the grant of food aid to India, our neighbour Pakistan did everything to dissuade USA from going ahead with their food aid plan.

The Indian enslavement by Britain happened on account of disunity displayed by Indian potentates, Hindu or Muslim. Pakistan-India distrust is an extension of the old disunity and again foreign interests will be the beneficiaries. When Indians realized that the British were bent on partition of India, they accepted partition in place of possible balkanization which was looming large. India with an understanding of history and power play between the victorious allies accepted immediate partition and freedom than a post-dated cheque of India's freedom without partition. Pakistan on the realization that their fond hopes had not been satisfied would want more chunk of India. One way to get it was to rely on the communists to succeed in making India a multi-national state often extolled by their theorists, they hoped then to shrink India to the bone and fish for some other parts in alliance with the communists. Churchill was the first to outline the hidden agenda of world domination by the communists and he warned all nations and nationalists from trusting the communist promises. Later, his views were confirmed by the insurrection by communists in Malaysia and Myanmar before the independence of these countries through the momentum generated by the Indian independence. Pakistan now leaned back on its last resort that of defeating India on a chosen front and detaching the state of Jammu & Kashmir for itself. The tribal assault with the fiction of neutrality of Pakistan army did not work the way it was supposed to and it only strengthened the bond of India with this Muslim majority Indian state. Pakistan now tried its luck with the alliances around the Soviet Union being manoeuvred by USA. Pakistan joined both SEATO and CENTO, and thought that it was ready (after the declaration of budding alliance with China cemented by giving them stolen chunk of J&K state in the North), for military adventure against India. It was also heartened by the poor performance of India in the north during the conversion of minor clashes in 1962 into large scale attack by the Chinese border guards. Pakistan opened the attack in 1965 by air strikes and then sending its armour across the western borders of India. Pakistan hoped to reach Delhi with the speed of its Patton tanks newly gifted by the USA to fight the spread of communism ! China also rattled its support of Pakistan allegedly driven to attack India in order to survive with dignity. In the battle of Khem Karan the whole countryside became a graveyard of Pakistani tanks. India showed its readiness to make a counter attack directly aiming at the capture of Lahore. Before the end of hostilities, the President of the Soviet Union had taken on the role of peace maker and invited the two sides to confer at Tashkent for signing a peace agreement. India did not obtain any direct advantage from the sacrifices it had made to counter the aggression. India desired that Pakistan would respond to the hand of friendship extended to it by India and to co-operate in the South Asia region.

India had now become interested in strengthening the Non-Aligned Movement and cared for the inclusion of many friendly countries from all continents and particularly the countries from the Middle East and wished to close the chapter of India-Pakistan war as early as possible. In the 1965 war with Pakistan, when, after the debacle of our border posts in the north at the hands of the Chinese, India could smash an invasion by the Pakistan army led by most modern tanks gifted to them by the USA, a simple explanation that could be offered was that China had no real reason to fight. The border skirmishes just went out of control of local military commanders and were soon put back on track. That episode had brought home to the Indian government many lessons in military preparedness and the need for adequate winter clothing and advance oil depots or superior infantry weapons and tactics for hilly terrain. The fight with Pakistan was different. It was a defensive battle against unprovoked aggression and a defeat could lead to the dismemberment of India. India regarded itself as a bastion of reason in the jungle of "might is right" and the prevailing climate of ganging up against a less militarily prepared nation. India's persistence in wooing friendship of Pakistan bore fruit only in the. 21st century after the terrorist attack on USA.

4.2 Military Dictatorship in Pakistan

With the death of Mr. Jinnah and the murder of Liaqat Ali Khan, democracy departed from Pakistan. They had a string of military dictators as Presidents or Prime Ministers with interludes of constitution drafting to suit the rulers in power. (This is the situation even now). A demand for a fresh plebiscite has existed all along in Sind and Baluchistan as well as in the tribal belt along the border with Afghanistan in the north. In 1958 President Mirza overriding the constitution appointed Gen. Ayub as Prime Minister and very soon the Prime Minister staged a coup to become the

President himself with all powers. Gen. Ayub had Bhutto as his loyal Prime Minister till 1969 when Gen. Ayub made room for Gen. Yahya Khan. Soon there would be another trial of arms with India and the liberation of East Pakistan as a new Bangladesh nation. This happened because Bhutto desired unquestioned power in West Pakistan which he could not have since Mujib-ul-Rehman was the majority leader of Pakistan under democratic elections. The Bengali speaking population was in majority in Pakistan and Bengali language had earlier been denied the status of a national language. The suppression of the movement for autonomy in East Pakistan led to a rebellion and with open assistance of the Indian army, the freedom fighters of the Bengali Mukti Vahini liberated East Pakistan. The Bangladesh flag was unfurled earlier by Mujib-ul-Rehman in a state election meeting leading to his imprisonment in a West Pakistani jail. He was later released to become the chosen president of independent republic of Bangladesh. When the hard pressed Pakistan army in Bangladesh could not be speedily reinforced directly across India, Pakistan attacked India from the west in a bid to go across. This only resulted in India sending its army to help the Bangladesh bid for liberation. The Pakistan army of occupation about 93,000 in number surrendered to the Indian forces and was repatriated to Pakistan after a period of confinement in India. India made no demands on Pakistan nor did it attempt to democratize the Pakistan government.

Mrs. Gandhi visited Dacca in March 1972 and signed a treaty of Peace, Friendship and Co-operation with Sheikh Mujibur Rehman. Complacency on the part of the victors cost Rehman his life in 1975. The Sheikh floated a new party "Krishak Sangrami League" losing his established popular base. He and his many relatives were gunned down by a coup carried out by some pro-Pakistan elements in the newly raised Bangladesh Army. The independent government of Bangladesh was thus destroyed.

The entrenched fanatics in positions of responsibility allowed the murderer junta to form the new government of coup leaders, while Begum Haseena Wajid, the succeeding head of the party of power who had survived the massacre, set about having new elections. The newly reorganized Bangladesh army however seized the government and Begum Haseena sat with reduced parliament strength in the opposition. Repeated rigged elections kept nationalists of the Awami Party in the opposition. North East India had many Hindu and Muslim refugees from Bangladesh. It was a problem there to absorb a large number of Bengali speaking refugees. In the truncated Pakistan, Bhutto strengthened his hold by dismissing the elected NWFP government but he lost to the next military dictator, Gen. Zia-ul-Haq in 1977. Soon after he was hanged for an alleged murder he had contrived during his climb to power. Bangladesh has found some comfort in the present democratic set-up under Begum Haseena. India supports Bengladesh in their quest for peaceful development. The common Bengali language with the Bengali population of North East India would count for more trade and commerce and ease in communications with India and particularly North East India.

4.3 Terrorism in Pursuit of National Ambitions

After the debacle in Bangladesh, Pakistan continued to allow its agency ISI to pursue terrorism against India. Terrorism was first practiced in the Indian state of J&K, its development and economic growth were deliberately thwarted by manipulating religious outrages against various communities and burning down of schools and nation building assets. Incessant rioting threw out the religious minorities of Hindus and Sikhs. The Kashmiri Pandits, the ancient residents of the state were forced to become refugees in their own country. Pakistan had acquired the skill of ethnic cleansing in their struggle for the formation of Pakistan. The ISI perpetrated terrorism now on the innocent people busy in their daily chores. There were terrorist attacks on busy markets and even legislatures in J&K and on temples and the Parliament in Delhi as well as near Ayodhya close to the Babri Mosque. There were bomb blasts in the markets and suburban trains of Mumbai, and in the bazars of Jaipur in Rajasthan.

4.4 Khalistan Card

India now got busy strengthening its Navy and Air Force since at the height of Bangladesh crisis, USA had dispatched a naval task force to the Bay of Bengal apparently in support of beleagured Pakistanis, but before it could clarify its intentions, Pakistan had signed the surrender documents regarding its army in Bangladesh, India devoted an all-out effort to defence research, atomic energy, rocketry and missile development.

Some Sikhs in India or residents abroad in England or Canada thought it a good moment to grab a part of the Punjab and try to form an independent Sikh state carved out of the Punjab. The ISI (secret service of Pakistan) became very active counting on the Sikh unrest. Pakistan started nuclear proliferation activity with China, and used clandestine purchases of atomic reactor components, auxiliary machines and electronics from private firms in USA and Europe and feverishly engaged itself by borrowed or stolen technology for making atomic weapons. Jihadi as well as Khalistani terrorism engineered by the ISI and the Khalistan activists increased both in J&K state as well as in other parts of India. Two Sikh bodyguards of the Indian Prime Minister, who were brain-washed to believe her to be instrumental in ordering clean up of Sikh rebellious elements from the Darbar Sahib at Amritsar, shot her at her official residence. Murder in the target country without declaration of hostilities has been a common practice of the intelligence agencies.

Guru Nanak was a prophet of human unity and peace of his times. He exposed the empty gestures that had crept into religious practices during that period. All truly religious greats like Baba Farid, Kabir, Amir Khusro and many saints and *Bhaktas* in India, have done the same. His teachings as well as uplifting messages and compositions of other saints, sufis and philosophers are enshrined in the Guru Granth Sahib, the holy book of the Sikhs. Guru Nanak and other Sikh Gurus taught in the common man's langauge and not in Sanskrit, the language of learned discourse of the Hindus. All the Sikh Gurus were Punjabees. A Hindu could easily become a follower of the Sikh Gurus without any declaration of leaving Hinduism. Hindus could accept any system that assured them spiritual advance. Guru Nanak was a contemporary of Babar when Islamic rule in India was being consolidated. Islam, a religion of peace and faith in a merciful God became a vehicle of Islamic domination in India. They looked down upon idolaterous Hindus and took particular pride in destruction of idols and looting of Hindu temples. The Sikh Gurus had seen atrocities being heaped on the Hindus of India. Later a *modus vivendi* was to develop and Hindus and Muslims were to build the Indian culture together. The Sikhs were taught by the Guru that Hindus and Muslims are all just human beings created by God. They demonstrated the ability to sacrifice for the pain of others and when necessary took up arms for the protection of the weak and to punish the evil doers. Guru Gobind Singh, the tenth Guru of the Sikhs personally suffered at the hands of Muslim zealots. He wrote his *Zafarnama* in Persian to the emperor at Delhi that unless his minions stop atrocities on the innocent public, the state should be prepared to face rebellion. Guru Gobind Singh was himself a military leader as well as a poet and writer in Sanskrit as well as Persian. He made rules to nip all backsliding among the Sikhs. He gave them a military face and enjoined rules of dress and conduct. He introduced baptism and the order of the Khalsa. Sikhs were to be a brotherhood in arms. The people of Punjab followed the Guru and the path of struggle and sacrifice till the Khalsa or the soldiers of the Guru were successful in the eviction of the fanatic rule of Mughals from the Punjab or the repeated effort of the invading tribal (neo-Muslims) allies from Kabul. Guru Gobind Singh believed in transmigration of soul and believed that he was a Yogi in his previous life and had practiced austerities worshipping the Almighty. The word *Bhagwati* in the Sikh prayer when written in the Persian script, reads as *Bhagoti* and it was interpreted as sword by the Sikh intellectuals. Many have distanced themselves from the Khalistani militants.

4.5 Hand of Co-operation and Friendship

India is certain to gain further from its current ordeal of terrorism. India happily joined USA in combating terrorism. The anti-terrorist activity also includes the participation of other friendly countries like Russia and China who are also intended victims of *jehadi* terrorism. Pakistan who had sponsored terrorists in the garb of Mujahideen and the Taliban has itself become a victim. Since it is still allowing the existence of a large number of terrorist training camps, it cannot be absolved from the taint of nurturing terrorism still.

Taiwan is still a second China which the Chinese have resolved to reunite. When India and Pakistan start pulling together, that would be the end of imperialism. The demise of *jehadi* terrorism will follow the consolidation of independent Afghanistan to which India has great affinity.

4.6 The Kashmir Standoff

After the Indo-Pakistan wars of 1947, 1965 and 1971, there was a limited war for clearing Pakistani infestation of Kargil heights within India. Terrorist attacks also occurred on the Indian Parliament and the Red Fort as well as other places in India. There was always a threat of Pakistan's nuclear capability, in case India responded more vigorously. The World Bank assisted India-Pakistan agreement for the sharing of the Punjab waters has been a great success. Pakistan still calls Indian control of Kashmir as a threat through river control warfare ! Through open aggression and nuclear blackmail, Pakistan has continued to occupy one-third of the Indian state of J&K. The United Nations Commission for India and Pakistan rejected the Pakistani view that the presence of Pakistani troops in the occupied Kashmir area be treated at par with the presence of Indian army in the Kashmir state which has been part of India by choice of the Kashmiris since the sixteenth century. Owen Dixon who had taken over as the UN representative in 1950 had said that the role of the tribes and the Pakistani army in the Kashmir conflict was contrary to international law. The Shimla Agreement ratified by the Pakistan National Assembly makes it a mutual obligation to arrive at a negotiated settlement of the Kashmir issue. The slogan of Islamic *jehad* in Kashmir and letting loose the *jehadi* terrorists of Pakistan and other distant countries in Kashmir for terrorizing the population and killing of civilian and military persons in ambush in an undeclared war of aggression is repugnant to the UN charter. The sworn statements of surrendered or apprehended terrorists point to their having been trained and brain-washed by the Pakistan army regulars among others. Many nations belonging to the organization of Islamic countries have exhorted in favour of peaceful resolution of the Indo-Pak problems. Pakistan has been given the major non-NATO ally status by the USA. Pranab Mukherjee, then India's Defence Minister, reacting to such reports stated in December 2004 that the supply of sophisticated weapons like F16 aircraft, missiles and naval surveillance aircraft to Pakistan would jeopardize the Indo-Pak peace process. Such weapons are not required for fighting terrorism.

India and Pakistan together can be a change agent for fast development of South Asia. According to leaders like late General A.I. Akram of Pakistan, India had an ambition to become a global power. Such views were expressed only to misguide their own people and to fuel fear among smaller nations of South Asia. India has openly espoused the cause of education and development in the third world. It would rather have all countries develop and contribute to prosperity. Development of countries in the post-modern world is dependent on ethical discipline, and application of science and technology along with the employment of better methods of organization and management. International development is not a zero sum game. Pakistani leaders had kept up a relentless anti-India campaign while siphoning off large quantities of arms and ammunition acquired from USA and Saudi Arabia ostensibly for anti-Soviet operations in Afghanistan for training and used by terrorists for operations in Asia and Europe.

Shireen Mazari of the Institute of Strategic Studies, Islamabad, argued that the nuclear option would restrain India from expanding any conflict to full scale war. Qazi Hussain Ahmed a religio-plitical leader of Pakistan exhorted the Bhutto Government in 1994 to develop nuclear weapons as a deterrent against India. The same year, Nawaz Sharif warned India that an attack on Pakistan could trigger a nuclear war. He also said that an escalation of the Kashmir crisis because of New Delhi's failure to surrender Kashmir to Pakistan was inevitable implying a naked nuclear threat. Pakistan's nuclear capability was thus declared to be tied to its position in Kashmir. Pakistan believed India to have no option but to suffer silently the drain on its resources by the low intensity terrorist operations against India staged from Pakistan or Pakistan occupied Kashmir. General Musharraf's gestures to clamp down on militant outfits in Pakistan proved to be illusory. The cat was out of the bag only when the militants challenged Musharraf's army in Lal Masjid at the centre of Islamabad. According to the July 2002 report of the International Crisis Group entitled "Pakistan Madarsas, Extremism, and Militancy", there were attempts only to direct militancy at targets outside Pakistan favoured by the state and dissuade them from creating instability within Pakistan. Pakistan's links with Al Qaeda have given credence to the view that militancy was always a preferred arm of Pakistan's establishment. The US State Department issued a categorical statement that their Deputy Secretary Armitage was given assurances by President Musharraf on June 6, 2002, that ending of infiltration across the line of control would be permanent. Building on such assurances to the USA, the Indian Prime Minister Dr. Manmohan Singh has in July 2007 expressed the hope that the line of control will soon become the line of peace or in other words the international frontier, which has so far been un-acceptable to both the countries. In fact such a solution was staring in the face of the UN since 1948. Only manoeuvring for self-interest of big powers thwarted a ready solution. Altaf Hussain, the leader of the Muttahida Qaumi Movement of Pakistan reinforced this idea in November 2004.

Terrorist training camps in POK (Pakistan Occupied Kashmir) are still functioning according to Indian intelligence gathered from surrendered or captured militants from places like Varanasi or Gujarat and Jaipur in India. The collusion between the ISI (the premier Pakistan military inter-service intelligence agency) and the fundamentalists in Bangladesh and Nepal is well known. In the long history of discussions on Kashmir, the first ever interaction of the All Party Hurriyat Conference with India's Prime Minister took place in New Delhi in September 2005 during which the Prime Minister emphasized the need for cessation of violence in Kashmir and an end to the infiltration of *jehadis* from across the LOC. which could automatically reduce the role of Indian armed forces in Kashmir. The Prime Minister reiterated his government's resolve to protect human rights and to ensure for the citizens in J&K a life of peace, self-respect and dignity.

4.7 Confidence Building Measures

Many initiatives to improve Indo-Pak relations have been taken by India. People to people relations surprisingly have been excellent in spite of deep hurts experienced by all during the partition riots. Perhaps due to the injustice perpetrated by the authorities in those days of alienation and saber rattling, inter-governmental relations plummeted. The I.K. Gujral government was the first one to set in motion confidence building measures. Atal Behari Vajpayee made the concrete gesture of undertaking a bus journey from Delhi to Lahore and signing a Declaration of Peace. The budding atmosphere of peaceful intentions was, however, smothered by the Kargil adventure of General Musharraf when as a fresh strategist he occupied Kargil heights on the Indian side of the line of control, which led to a large military effort to get this area vacated from Pakistani soldiers sitting on heights overlooking the Indian road for supplies to Kashmir from Indian cantonments in the plains. A terrorist attack on the Indian Parliament worsened the situation. There were astounding statements from persons in high places in Pakistan that even if the Kashmir issue was resolved, friendship between Pakistan and India would remain elusive. It may be recalled that India had proposed a bilateral agreement on "no first use of nuclear weapons" to no avail. One felt that offers of talks by General Musharraf could only be a ploy to further implement new aggressions on India. Pakistan's continued stockpiling of lethal weapons only underscored the lack of confidence in Indian efforts to create an ambience of peace, cooperation and prosperity in the subcontinent. What was urgently required was perhaps the re-establishment of democracy in Pakistan which alone could give credence to people's desire in the Indian subcontinent for peaceful coexistence. President Musharraf's stand off with the country's Chief Justice who proved his grasp of people's requirements was one of the most critical events in Pakistan's history. The reinstatement of the Chief Justice and other judges of the Federal Court has saved the day for Pakistan.

In order to encourage people to people contacts, a right move has been made to open Srinagar-Muzaffarabad bus route. A Lahore-Amritsar bus service was also introduced. But due to building tensions, it has been discontinued. It was intended to encourage trade and economic cooperation. In spite of Pakistani assurances, Pakistani soldiers have been firing across the LOC causing damage to life and property on the Indian side while the military commanders feign ignorance of such happenings. There are instances when infiltrating terrorist squads have been provided artillery cover. But the Indian Prime Minister holds Pakistan's leaders in high regard claiming that here is an opportunity to arrive at a settlement. Contrary to expectations, Pakistan has been less generous in granting visas to Indian artists and entertaining groups.

4.8 Rapprochement

When Prime Minister Dr. Manmohan Singh and President Pervez Musharraf met at Havana against the backdrop of the NAM summit, they renewed the strategic peace agreement between India and Pakistan. They reiterated their commitment and determination to implement the joint statements of January 6, 2004; September 24, 2004; April 18, 2005; and September 14, 2005. Both leaders condemned all acts of terrorism and agreed that terrorism was a scourge that needs to be effectively dealt with. The leaders agreed that the peace process must be maintained and its success was important for both the countries and the future of the entire region.

They agreed on the joint search for mutually acceptable peacefully negotiated settlement of all issues including that of J&K state, boundary of the Sir Creek or the Siachen issue. Vacation of the glacier would be possible only after a full agreement on Kashmir. As per the UN Convention, the deepest point in a marsh would be a guide for the boundary. If a demarcated boundary is not submitted to the UN by 2009, the waters are likely to be converted into international boundary.

According to economists, the granting of the MFN status to India in trading would generate tax revenues instead of losing the same to smuggling. Agricultural and industrial products would gain access to a much larger market. Fundamentalism and the *jehadi* mentality has become a stumbling block in Pakistan's progress. Pursuing his agenda of peace, Prime Minister, Dr. Manmohan Singh has suggested to turn Siachen, the world's highest battleground into a mountain of peace. There would be first authentication of location of present posts held by both sides so that there is no adverse occupation after withdrawal of troops after general understanding.

Towards energy security of both the countries, it is heartening to see both seriously considering the project of a gas pipeline from Iran to India across Pakistan. India has offered to sell diesel to Pakistan. This proposed 2600 km gas pipeline has a rival in ADB sponsored pipeline, the Turkmenistan-Afghanistan-Pakistan-India line. As neighbours, Pakistan and India could open their air space for civil aviation for flights terminating in either country. The public of both countries has welcomed Indian aid to earthquake ravaged parts of Pakistan occupied territories, India's offer of free medical treatment to children from Pakistan and the establishment of links between the two coastguard authorities to avoid undue hardship to fishermen caught fishing in wrong territorial waters. The two countries could augment their embassy staff so that the embassies can handle more travel between the two when the rail, road and ferry links are increased.

In recent elections in Pakistan, a People's Party led coalition has taken over. The slain Begum Benazir Bhutto's husband, Asif Ali Zardari is the President. General Pervez Musharraf has been forced to shed military uniform and give up the presidency, though he expects to return soon from his sojourn abroad.

4.9 Issues Other Than those of Kashmir

Pakistan's defence doctrine is entirely India centred. Islamization of Pakistan army is continuing since its start by Gen. Zia-ul-Haq. The democratic regime may have to create a secular environment first to prepare for a new era, allowing coexistence of all. All should benefit from new scientific discoveries and explanations. India and Pakistan have to bid good-bye to the past of suspicion and strife. It is never too late to engage in cooperative efforts to alleviate poverty, illiteracy and disease and to build further on our common cultural heritage. Pakistan's adoption of no first use of nuclear weapons will reassure its neighbours as India has already adopted this discipline. This would be genuine statesmanship. To cement the budding good relations, India could count on Pakistan's support for its deserved permanent membership of the UN Security Council. India has an open invitation to the developing countries to its capabilities in the emerging technologies and nuclear power generation. India is a secular country having more Muslims in its fold than the entire population of Pakistan. Indian Muslims are loyal to the motherland and are equal partners in the democratic polity of the country. Even more reliance will be placed on individual merit than at present when the colonial legacy of political rights being based on caste and creed is slowly being dismantled. We have to fight together terrorism, fanaticism and fundamentalist exclusivism to ensure peace and plenty in the subcontinent.

4.10 USA for Thaw in India Pakistan Relations

After the terrorists attacked the trade towers in New York, the indifference of USA to terrorists in the world ceased and India-Pakistan relations assumed new importance since India became an ally against terrorism while USA already claimed Pakistan to be its first ally against terrorism. The USA now hoped that India and Pakistan will close their ranks and not pull in opposite directions when they are to fight the terrorists together. USA continued to give arms aid to Pakistan but also exhorted that country to abide by the Shimla agreement and resolve the Kashmir problem bilaterally. India and USA also talked about strategic convergence between the two countries and prepared a draft understanding for nuclear collaboration for peaceful purposes. India pursued this change of attitude of the West and intensified its diplomacy for the success of its confidence building measures with Pakistan.

In January 2002, Gen. Musharraf declared that he would take measures against terrorists operating from Pakistani soil against India. India believes that Pakistan is moving leisurely regarding terrorist organizing cells in India and giving them training and arms. On June 24, 2002, President Musharraf reiterated that he would put a stop to infiltration into India from POK. A well known Pakistani columnist described Pakistan's relationship with the US as one of dependence and deceit. Pranab Mukherjee, reacting to continuing arms aid by USA, said on December 12, 2004 that the supply of sophisticated weapons: F-16 aircraft, lethal missiles and surveillance aircraft could jeopardize the peace process between Pakistan and India. The leader of the MQM movement of Pakistan has opined that conversion of the LOC into an international border may suit all concerned. The two sides have to come to an understanding by whittling down their claims, this is the emerging view in many conclaves. Pakistan's elite now running the government are being confronted by the true anarchical nature of the terrorists when they started terrorist activities within Pakistan, e.g. happenings in Lal Masjid in the capital of Pakistan or practically a rebellion in the areas adjoining Afghanistan infested by international terrorists. The loud propaganda against Pakistan's close embrace of the US in the anti-terrorism activity is still occurring.

In September 2005, the All Parties Hurriat Conference, an organization of pro-Pakistan politicians of Kashmir first held discussions with President Musharraf and then for the first time sought a meeting with Dr. Manmohan Singh, the Prime Minister of India, who assured them that as soon as violence was forsaken by the *jehadists* in Kashmir, India will certainly reduce the army presence there. The package of confidence building measures and opening of more rail and bus links have been welcomed by all Kashmiris. India would welcome the start again of trade route to Central Asia by road or air across Pakistan.

4.11 Terrorism

India has been afflicted with terrorism waged by Islamic fundamentalists secure in their protection from Pakistan. The world took notice of such international terrorism only when Trade Towers in New York were attacked. Today's terrorists are well trained, motivated brilliantly up to self-destruction. The medieval examples of Turkish Jan Nissaries, Japanese Kamikaze bombers, Rajput Joharites exist. Most others were champions of a lost cause, but modern terrorists have almost no cause when they operate in democratic secular countries like India, USA or Russia. The success against Arab Palestine and secular Yugoslavia had emboldened them. Riches from smuggling, narcotics trade and mafia banking financed them. They are happy to invent causes like the isolated contentment of the Maldives or the lost empire of the Sikhs.

The most senseless and wild attack was on the Indian Parliament by the Pakistan linked terrorists and most devastating attack was by a similar outfit loyal to Osama-bin-Laden on the American Trade Towers. J&K state of India has borne low intensity war by proxy infiltrators across the Line of Control to perpeterate outrages in India and in Kashmir.

5 Foreign Policy

5.1 Policy of Coexistence and Respect for National Rights

India won freedom from colonial rule in August 1947. It had already gained recognition as a nation when accepted as a member of the UNO in 1945. Just before Independence, Jawaharlal Nehru convened the Asian Relations Conference at New Delhi in March 1947 where he declared that, for peace, all countries must be free and all human beings must be free in the exercise of their rights regarding security and opportunity. India's vision of the world has been that particularly the emerging free nations would be democratic and putting aside mutual distrust would build a new cooperating world. Policy of coexistence includes non-alignment and friendly relations with all countries.

Unfortunately, the newly independent countries had been the testing ground for all kinds of divisive ideologies encouraged by the colonialists under the policy of divide and rule. An Islamic *Jihad* party under the label of Muslim League had been created and encouraged to propagate a two nation theory for India. India was divided on the eve of independence into a Muslim majority part in the east and west, and the rest of India. The Muslim League went one step forward and prepared pogroms for non-Muslims, *i.e.* the Hindus and Sikhs in the Muslim majority parts. Retaliatory pogroms occurred against Muslims in the Punjab and Bihar. More than ten million people fled from their homes and became refugees in India or in Pakistan. The Indian authorities curbed the rioters while in Pakistan there was abetment to loot and murder as the *Mullahs* held Islam to allow despoiling of *kafirs* ! In the same vein, there was an attack by Muslim tribals with express nod from Pakistan army on Kashmir to force it to join Pakistan and not to India as was expected from the partition arrangements finalized by UK. Indian counter response to the raiders after securing the Srinagar airport by para-drops was to chase the raiders back, but before the entire state could be cleared, under international pressure from the imperialist creators of division of India, Nehru clamped a cease fire and thought it fit to complain to the UN under the delusion of own creation that the UN Security Council will do justice. The UN in clear partiality to Western powers treated the matter not of aggression on a member-state but as a territorial dispute between two neighbouring states. The Kashmir problem has been dealt earlier while dealing with India-Pakistan distrust. To have an alternative supplier of military hardware in the face of growing solidarity seen between the Western powers and Pakistan, India developed further cooperation with the Soviet Union. We were lukewarm with criticism of takeover of Hungary by the Soviet bloc but had reacted vociferously against the attempted takeover of the Suez Canal by Britain and France.

We preferred Suez Canal to remain an international artery outside the clutches of imperialist powers. International Law needed some basic foundation for the modern world. *Panchsheel* or the five principles of peaceful coexistence were first formally enunciated in the agreement on trade and intercourse between the Tibet region of China and India signed on April 29, 1954. The five principles meant mutual respect for each other's territorial integrity and sovereignty, mutual non-aggression, mutual non-interference, equality and mutual benefit, and peaceful coexistence. According to the two Prime Ministers, the ideology of *Panchsheel* would help in creating an area of peace that could be enlarged to lessen the chances of war and to strengthen the cause of peace. *Panchsheel* was incorporated in the ten principles of international peace and cooperation enunciated by the Bandung Conference of 29 Afro-Asian nations held at Bandung in April 1955. In December 1957, the UN General Assembly emphasized its relevance when it unanimously adopted a resolution on peaceful coexistence presented by India, Yugoslavia and Sweden. The Non-Aligned Conference in 1961 accepted *Panchsheel* as the core of the movement. The essence of *Panchsheel* is the non-use of power, and the embrace of tolerance. Reiterating this concept, Prime Minister Mrs. Indira Gandhi said in her speech at the seventh NAM Summit in New Delhi in March 1983,"Only with coexistence can there be any existence. We regard non-interference and non-intervention as basic laws of international behaviour." India-China international border is still a matter of dispute though the principles and historical facts that should determine it are now agreed upon. *Panchseel* had a jolt when China escalated the border skirmishes into a regular armed incursion into India in 1962 but beat a hasty withdrawal after a unilateral ceasefire when it found no preparation for war by India, and quoted its reborn zeal for belief in *Panchsheel.* The brief India-China encounter had far greater lessons for India. India became more conscious of real politics and need for developing better defence capability as in acquiring nuclear weapons and assuring some deterrence on potential aggressors. After the visit of Rajiv Gandhi, the Indian Prime Minister to China in 1988, a joint press communiqué declared, "These (*Panchsheel*) principles also constitute the basic guidelines for the establishment of a new international political order and the new international economic order. Both sides agreed that their common desire was to restore, improve and develop India-China good neighbourly and friendly relations on the basis of these principles. The spirit of this declaration was reiterated during the return visit in 1991 of the Chinese Premier Li Peng. India had helped Communist China in the UN in getting recognition and in replacing Kuomintang as a permanent member of the Security Council, on merits of the case and not as a deal with anyone.

5.2 Non-Alignment

In foreign policy non-alignment became the main plank in view of pressing need of peace and uninterrupted development, and the world being pulled incessantly towards war by the opposing pulls of capitalist West and communist Soviet bloc further strengthened by the communist success in China. Nehru explained that by remaining non-aligned we can use such influence as we may possess in the cause of world peace. He did not see any positive value in becoming a part of the manoeuvring that was going on in the world. India would develop closest relations with all the countries. Besides consolidating India's integrity *vis-à-vis* Pakistan who aspired to despoil India of some territory, India would establish friendly relations with both USA and USSR. Pakistan had already gifted a portion of Pakistan occupied territory of Kashmir to China, though China had stipulated the finalization of the donation only after India and Pakistan sort out their rights over Kashmir. As India refused to align with USA and the British against the Soviets and the Chinese, the United States became suspicious of India. Indian refusal to sign the Japanese peace treaty or to side with the US sponsored UN resolution on the Korean conflict caused further alienation of US policy-makers about India but the sincerity of India about world peace won it appreciation and trust at the international level. General Thimmaya of India was designated Chairman of the neutral nations repatriation commission for ascertaining the wishes of about 150,000 North Korean and Chinese prisoners of war captured by the UN forces in the Korean conflict. India also made mediatory efforts between France and Vietnam following the latter's defeat at Dien Bien Phu. India was named as chairman of the UN Control Commission dealing with Laos, Cambodia and Vietnam, with Poland and Canada as other members.

With the Western powers' antipathy towards Indian defence needs, India had to turn to the Soviet Union. A new era of close and cordial relations ensued after the exchange of visits by Nehru to the Soviet Union and of Khrushchev and Bulganin to India in 1955. By late 1950s, the Chinese gave hints of grabbing Indian territory of Arunachal Pradesh. By 1959, attempts of the Dalai

Lama to maintain the autonomy of Tibet failed to the extent that he together with his entourage fled to India seeking political asylum. China interpreted this as Indian interference and retaliated by increased patrolling along the India-Tibet border (McMahon line not recognized so far by the Chinese) and soon border clashes were converted into full scale attack across the northern borders of India by the Chinese border guards who speedily overran the Indian base at Bom de La and crossed over to Tezpur. The Chinese soon realized that India was not preparing for aggression against China and had been needlessly antagonized. There was a unilateral ceasefire and withdrawal of the Chinese forces to a line of actual control just south of the McMahon line. Pakistan, taking advantage of the situation forged strategic and defence relations with China. India's domestic economic policies appeared to USA as being opposed to free market economy. India's opposition to military alliances and the US attitude of treating India and Pakistan as equal disputants in Kashmir kept India aloof from USA. President Eisenhower visited India in 1959. Food and economic assistance to India and educational and cultural exchanges between the two countries emerged. He was impressed by the public goodwill visible in India for the USA.

India recognized the Fidel Castro regime in Cuba. India favoured dismantling of Cuban missiles but did not fully support the USA in the Cuban Missile Crisis. A wide recognition of the Non-aligned Movement among the third world countries was not considered good for western interests. India also favoured universal disarmament counter to US perception. In spite of tremendous Western influence, a number of popular African leaders fell under the spell of non-alignment. Nehru, Nasser, Tito, Soekarno and Nkrumah were the principal leaders of the movement. There was a setback due to war between China and India in 1962 and Nehru died soon after in 1964. Besides joining SEATO and CENTO, Pakistan had also become an active member of the organization of Islamic countries. The Pakistani leaders became more assertive about Kashmir. The US had provided massive military assistance to Pakistan. In 1965, Pakistan attacked India in the Rann of Kutch and soon after in Kashmir, but a spirited counter attack by India under the policy formulated by Lal Bahadur Shastri who had succeeded Nehru, saved the day for India. Indian forces badly mauled the Pakistan launched Patton tanks at Khemkaran in the Punjab. Pakistan had to pull back its forces poised to attack Kashmir to save its main territory around Lahore. Pakistan's attack using American arms donated to fight communism could not have taken place without prior clearance with the USA. The Soviet leader Kosygin convened a meeting between Ayub Khan, the military dictator of Pakistan and Lal Bahadur Shastri, the Indian Prime Minister, at Tashkent after a ceasefire. The parties agreed to vacate each other's territories occupied during the war and Pakistan was to agree to sort out Kashmir problem only by peaceful negotiations with India. This war practically put an end to the saber rattling against India by Pakistan on the strength of their military alliances.

On the sudden death of Shastri at Tashkent on account of a heart attack, Mrs. Indira Gandhi became the Indian Prime Minister. She had an eventful rule. There was a rebellion in the Eastern wing of Pakistan when an elected majority leader, Mujib-ur-Rehman hailing from the eastern wing was not allowed to become the Prime Minister of Pakistan since during the elections he had campaigned for autonomous East Pakistan and he was imprisoned as a rebel. Pakistan tried to suppress the rebellious East Bengalis who after getting military assistance and recognition from India, were victorious. The Pakistan army, 93000 troops, surrendered to the Indian commander in the field, Jagjit Singh Aurora. West Pakistan came under full control of Bhutto as Prime Minister and soon had a string of new military dictators, who first hanged the Prime Minister for an old political murder. Mrs. Gandhi strengthened India's friendship with the Soviet Union. She also improved Indian relations with neighbours like Nepal, Sri Lanka, Bhutan, Afghanistan, Myanmar and Maldives. More substance was put into Indian relations with Iran and some African countries. India had already negotiated the peaceful merger of the French possessions of certain pockets on the East and the West coast of India, but since the Portuguese were not forthcoming in peace, they were ousted from Goa and small villages of Daman and Diu on the Gujarat coast of India after rebellion by their subjects with the tacit support of India. Indira Gandhi's control over Indian territories after the liberation of Bangladesh was more complete than that of anyone ever in Indian history.

5.3 Non-Proliferation Treaty

India did not sign the NPT as it discriminated between powers who had nuclear weapons of their own in 1968 and others. The others were prohibited to have such weapons or acquiring the technology to have them. The USA reacted by refusal to supply nuclear fuel after the expiry of the then existing agreement. Canada under US pressure also went back on its obligations with regard to the Rajasthan Atomic Power Project. This treaty has proved to be a most ludicrous treaty in spite of its important subject of great interest to the whole world desirous of freedom from the nuclear threat from the bomb owning countries. The treaty aimed to reduce the spread of atom bomb making technology or the technology to produce fissionable uranium of high purity. The plain historical fact is that some of the nations which possessed the technologies, busily spread the same to their favourite nations. In the case of Pakistan, a retired nuclear energy chief Abdul Qadeer Khan started a private business to spread the technology and to procure required special instruments and machines under false pretenses or under diplomatic immunity.

India should have been judged by past performance. India has never been guilty of encouraging proliferation, even when it has progressed alternative technologies for producing weapon grade fissionable materials. To counter the threat of atomic weapons we require complete disarmament or at least holding bombs and fissionable material only in trust for and under the control of International Atomic Energy Authority which was already constituted. Slowly USA has been coming around to India's logical stand and is willing to make an exception by getting into cooperation with India for civilian production and use of atomic energy without India being a member of the NPT. Indian adherence to the same in spirit unlike some existing signatories is widely recognized. At present, Iran's case is on the anvil. Iran also desired freedom to proceed as per its national interest and not tied down to the provisions of the NPT. India favours adjustment in the treaty to be signed by Iran in the light of its past performance in such matters and record of responsible behaviour. One must also bear in mind the historical might and civilizational influence of centuries of Iranian empire in Asia. India and Pakistan are together negotiating a gas pipeline deal with Iran. There was a stalemate on Indian and US positions regarding signing of the NPT, but there is some movement for more cooperation in the production of atomic energy for civil use and a comprehensive pioneering agreement is in sight.

5.4 International Cooperation

During the sixties, India started to take greater interest in International Economic Cooperation. India became a founding member of UNCTAD and the group of 77. India has been in the forefront of all international endeavours of the UN. India was an active partner in UN conferences on oceanography, on international law of the sea, or for laws dealing with space exploration. In principle, we are for international accord for UN governance through its member-nations. India assisted whole-heartedly and loyally all UN peace keeping operations, *e.g.* in Congo, in the Gaza Strip, Cyprus and Lebanon. In 1974, India and USA signed an agreement to strengthen their bilateral relations and decided to establish a joint commission for multi-directional cooperation. The visit of Moshe Dayan, the Israeli leader in 1978 was indicative of a shift in India's policy. Only in 1992, formal diplomatic relations have become a reality. Indian relations with Arab countries for liberation of Palestine have to stay unharmed. India expressed her dismay at Soviet intervention in Afghanistan but has welcomed renewal of Afghan independence after the defeat of the Taliban, the arch fundamentalists and demolishers of the Buddha statues in Bamian hills in Afghanistan. India and Pakistan are both allies of US in the campaign for the eradication of terrorism. USA and India have been the major targets of Islamic *jihad*, and now Pakistan is also targeted.

Mrs. Gandhi paid an official visit to US in 1982 when US supported an approximate assistance of $ 2 billion per annum from the international banking channels. The non-aligned and Commonwealth summits met in Delhi in 1983. Cooperation with the ASEAN group was sought as well as with the gulf countries. Rajiv Gandhi, son of Mrs. Gandhi was directly sworn in as Prime Minister after the assassination of his mother. He became a most effective and popular Prime Minister. The world political climate had also begun changing. There was a détente in Cold War signified by the understanding between Gorbachev and Reagen after Soviet Union decided to back out in a star war challenge. Gorbachev had become fascinated by the rate of development of the non-communist world. He decided to democratize the Soviet political order and liberalize the Soviet economy, dismantling various controls and inhibitions. He propounded the new concepts for the communists of *glasnost* (transparency) and *perestroika* (restructuring). He also decided to conclude the unfortunate involvement in Afghanistan and decided to leave the Afghans to their own devices. The alliance against the Soviet presence first allowed the Mujahideen and then the Taliban faction to seize power and when they soon found that the Taliban were most unpopular with peace loving Afghans, the allies laboured to put the genie of the Taliban back into the bottle. The Taliban are now active in the difficult terrain between settled area of North West Pakistan and the government controlled area of the Afghans. India and Afghans have continued their cooperation and trust and India would do much more for Afghan friends if they get transit facility for the purpose across Pakistan. The Taliban are out to bite the hand of Pakistan that had raised and trained them. Rajiv Gandhi undertook to reassure India's neighbourhood that India had no hegemonic ambitions. He demonstrated this by advising the Tamils to be satisfied with an autonomous state within Sri Lanka.

The Delhi declaration of Rajiv and Gorbachev on November 27, 1986 was a landmark that emphasized abjuring of violence and intimidation, inequality, oppression and discrimination. They stressed the need for rechannelising the resources from armaments to social and economic development. Both leaders called for destruction of nuclear arsenals and barring of all weapons from outer space. Cooperation between India and the Soviet Union reached a high level. Unfortunately the Soviet Union was not prepared yet for Gorbachev's revolution and it disintegrated through the desire of the common people to escape from the yoke of central direction. Rajiv Gandhi's visit to Beijing in December 1988 contributed a great deal in expanding Sino-Indian mutual trust. In an official visit to Pakistan, Rajiv Gandhi sought to impress on his counterpart Benazir Bhutto that Kashmir's accession to India was culturally, politically and historically final and non-negotiable. In the special session of the UN General Assembly, Rajiv Gandhi presented an action plan for a nuclear free, non-violent world order and a proposal for complete disarmament. There was wide support in the UN for his proposals.

Rajiv Gandhi participated in the Non-Aligned Summits in 1986 and 1989 and took a leading part in the establishment of an Africa Fund. India was chosen to be the Chairman of this trust fund. In the inaugural meeting leading to the creation of the South Asian Association of Regional Cooperation (SAARC) in December 1985, he was hopeful that the cooperation relying on the support of other countries will bring peace and progress to the region. The Association is likely to gain steam once the current thaw in India-Pakistan relations matures into cooperation.

5.5 Indian View of Important Pending Problems

Indian ambitions are non-hegemonic. She does not wish to become a solitary pole, firmly believing that all problems can reach a solution by discussion and mutual accommodation. The chief issue now is democratization of the UN. Pending further discussions and comprehensive steps towards its actualization is disarmament, handing over all nuclear and other WMDs to UN established cantonments. A related problem is to suppress terrorism and to reassure minorities and tiny communities that their aspirations will not be neglected by the larger community. Health, education and sufficient income for a contented life have to become universal by the active cooperation of all people. The USA by unilaterally attacking Iraq and occupying it under the unfounded charge of indulging in collecting WMD has preempted a just handling of the situation by dialogue. Iran and Iraq have been friends of India for a long time and we feel, that when allowed to act freely, these two will modernize Islam and bring it back to the path of peace and reason which it consistently illumined in the past.

India, South Africa and Brazil — one country each from Asia, Africa and South America, showed a new direction in international relations by forming IBSA with a focus on alleviation of hunger and poverty, ensuring sustainable development and expanding trade among the three countries. A joint statement was issued affirming that the three countries would be moulding their foreign policy in the light of their discussions and following strictly moral standards.

5.6 India-Russia Friendship

Globalization received an impetus with the disintegration of the Soviet Union. Russia showed dependence on western technology which resulted in countries like India with structural and friendship ties to the former USSR to look elsewhere. USA pressurized Russia not to supply cryogenic engines for the Indian space programme, though the supplying firm, Glavkosmos, had already delivered a substantial portion of the technology. Since the bulk of Indian frontline defence equipment could not now be upgraded or replaced by the Western sources, the need for reestablishing supply line from Russia was paramount. The Moscow declaration signed in 1994 underscored the special concerns of multi-ethnic states like Russia and India. Among the several agreements, an agreement on military and technical cooperation was significant. Prime Minister H.D. Deve Gowda's visit to Moscow in 1997 resulted in negotiating a deal for India to purchase $ 1.5 billion worth of fighter aircraft and other equipment. In October 2000, Vladimir Putin successor to President Yeltsin and the Indian Prime Minister agreed to transform the vision of strategic partnership into one befitting the expected multipolar world order. They also saw the relevance of bilateral cooperation between the three nations—Russia, China and India — at a natural pace. Among the agreements signed was one relating to Russian assistance in an Indian Lunar Mission. Both desired to strengthen the UN. The energy and industry (small and medium) sectors have great scope for mutual cooperation. India and Russia can also together further strengthen the WTO.

President Putin has vigorously held that India's permanent membership of the Security Council should include the right of veto. Putin evinced his interest to collaborate with India in civilian uses of nuclear energy. Russia has undertaken to provide four nuclear power plants at Kundankulam in Tamil Nadu State and Russia promised to give these plants perpetual supply of nuclear fuel unconditionally. In the past India has received great help from the Soviet Union and friendship with Russia is a continuation of that understanding. Russia is second only to USA as an arms exporter. During the first visit of President Putin to India, deals for supply of equipment worth $ 3 billion were made that included supply of Airborne Warning and Control Systems, submarines, Helix early warning helicopters, helicopters, tanks, surveillance and fire control radars, naval missiles. Aircraft carrier and MIG-29 KUB aircraft for use on the carrier will be supplied after further price negotiations.

The recent setting up of a consignment warehouse and a service centre in India will go a long way for an uninterrupted supply of spare parts and maintenance of equipment of Russian origin. Joint production projects are also envisaged, *e.g.* for the supersonic cruise missile. Russia has raised no hurdles for the sale of 60 metric tonnes of fuel for the Tarapur Atomic Power Station so that it could continue to function with safety. India-Russia trade is likely to triple by 2010.

5.7 Friendly Relations with Russia

We will give a brief step by step development of India-Russia relations:

(a) Stalin saw India and Pakistan firmly in the capitalist camp and avoided making policy a choice between India and Pakistan. The Soviet delegate was absent for example from the Security Council when the voting came up after discussions on the Kashmir issue in 1948 and 1949. USA offered military and economic assistance to Pakistan which soon became a member of the SEATO and CENTO and an active ally of USA. Pakistan had already offered a base in the Gilgit area to USA. The Indian and the Soviet approaches were similar on issues like disarmament, anti-colonialism and peace. Khrushchev repeatedly affirmed the Soviet support to India on the Kashmir issue.

Following the Chinese aggression against India in 1962, the Soviet leaders criticised the Chinese party as endangering all achievements of civilization. After the Indo-Pak war of 1965, the Soviet President facilitated the peace treaty. The Soviet Union had started supplying some arms and equipment to Pakistan in 1969 but soon after, this was stopped. On the other hand they warned Pakistan not to persist in a reign of terror in East Pakistan (now independent Bangladesh). They noted the deluge of refugees into India forcing India to assist the Bengal rebels.

The USA desired no interference with Pakistan for its actions within own territory. Soviet Veto blocked US resolution in support of Pakistan. In 1982, during her visit to Moscow, Prime Minister Indira Gandhi expressed her opinion that there should be withdrawal of Soviet troops from Afghanistan. In March 1984, India finalized the deal for the purchase and manufacture of MIG 27 and MIG 29 with the Soviet Union.

(b) *East Bengal Revolt against Pakistani oppression :* Soviet leaders issued a warning to Pakistan against their reign of terror in East Pakistan. UN intervention in favour of Pakistan was nipped in the bud by Soviet veto. Khrushchev repeatedly affirmed the Soviet support to India on Kashmir issue. India signed a treaty of peace and friendship on August 9, 1971 with the Soviet Union. The debacle of Pakistan in the 14-day struggle brought about the creation of a new nation state of Bangladesh. In 1982, Mrs. Indira Gandhi gave her opinion as a true friend that the Sovicts should withdraw their forces from Afghanistan. The Indian and the Soviet wishes had common features like disarmament, anti-colonialism and peace.

(c) *Chinese aggression and revolt in East Pakistan:* Following the Chinese aggression on India in 1962, F. Kozlov, a Soviet leader criticized the Chinese for playing with fire and endangering all achievements of human civilization.

(d) *Gorbachev and Rajiv Gandhi at the helm.* Gorbachev and Rajiv Gandhi concluded an agreement on guidelines for trade and for cooperation in science and technology. After the state visit to Delhi of President Gorbachev, Rajiv Gandhi made a statement in the Parliament that the USSR had joined India in a common vision of a nuclear weapons free and non-violent world following the ideas of Gandhi and Lenin. In the sphere of defence there was continuous flow of supplies. A nuclear powered submarine was leased to the Indian navy. The leaders ageed to cooperate in vital matters like disarmament and development. Inequality, oppression and discrimination were considered immoral and impermissible.

A fall out of Gorbachev's *glasnost* and *perestroika* was globalization. The new world order set the agenda for India-Russia bilateral relations. Globalization received an impetus from the collapse of the USSR. There was temporary breakdown of the commercial and financial arrangements. The Yeltsin regime in Russia stopped Russian sale of dual use technology items to India since India had not signed the NPT. Since the bulk of frontline battle equipment in India, purchased from the Soviet Union could not be upgraded or replaced by Western industry, the need for re-establishing the supply line from the communist independent states of Europe or Asia was paramount. The visit of Prime Minister P.V. Narasimha Rao to Moscow, in June 1994 underscored the strategic aspects of Indo-Russian relations. The Moscow declaration also mentioned the growing threat of terrorism to multi-ethnic states. Indo-Russian strategic and defence cooperation had been confirmed by new treaty of friendship and cooperation in 1992. Periodic meetings of a joint commission expanded the areas of activity. Prime Minister I.K. Gujral signed an agreement on joint liner service along Novorosssk-Mumbai/Chennai route.

(e) *Restoration of Strategic Cooperation* : Yevgeny Primakov chose India for his first visit abroad as Russia's Foreign Minister. He advocated Russia-India-China collaboration. But India had yet to resolve the border problem with China. President Yeltsin gave a commitment to complete an old deal for the supply of two light water nuclear power plants of 1000 MW each to be built in Tamil Nadu. The visit of Prime Minister Vajpai to Russia in November 2003 became another landmark in the strategic relationship. Both countries proposed earliest restoration of the sovereignty of Iraq. Among the accords that were signed, one related to space research including Russian assistance in the Indian Lunar Mission. President Putin reiterated that cross border terrorism must cease and the terrorist infrastructure in Pakistan must be dismantled for peace in South Asia.

(f) *Vajpai's address at the Russian Academy of Sciences :* Vajpai stressed the interest of both countries in the evolution of multi-polar world based on cooperative security. Vajpai acknowledged the Russian support for India's permanent membership of the Security Council. Vajpai said that terrorism was threatening the territorial integrity of both India and Russia. According to Putin, the same terrorist and extremist organizations were involved from the Philippines to Kosovo including Kashmir, Afghanistan and Chechenya. In his keynote address at the joint meeting of Indian and Russian business persons in Moscow on November 13, 2003, Prime Minister Vajpai described Russian and Indian economies as having tremendous potential for growth. The long standing multi-faceted bilateral agreement with Russia is the firm base on which modern economic edifice is being built. Russia has emerged as a leading supplier of energy and India is a fastest growing market for the same. There is also great potential for cooperation in the small and medium enterprises. The cooperation can span training, exchange of experts, supply of machinery and equipment. There can be contracts for turnkey execution of projects. India supported Russia's accession to the WTO. India and Russia have developed strong bonds of friendship over many decades. Economic partnership provides secure underpinning.

5.8 India-Russia Affinity of Minds

The visit of Vladimir Putin to New Delhi in December 2004 was another milestone.

Putin asserted vigorously that India's membership of the Security Council should be with full rights, including the right to veto. India and Russia adhered to the common ideals of secularism, democracy, rule of law, cultural diversity and pluralism. India is a crucial factor for stability in the region and in the world as a whole. Russia would like India to play an important role in international affairs.

The fourth official visit of Putin to India in January 2007 reflected a genuine consensus. The nine agreements which were signed underscored a message. Putin agreed to collaborate with India in the development of civilian nuclear energy. Russia has undertaken to provide four nuclear power plants at Kundankulam in Tamil Nadu state. Russia would also construct nuclear power plants at new sites without imposing any Russian specific conditions. Russia would also assure perpetual supply of fuel irrespective of any other differences that may arise between the two countries. Russia would of give free access to India to the navigation signals of the Global Navigation Satellite System for peaceful purposes. During the first visit, arms commission was upgraded from the Secretary level to the Minister level. India purchased sophisticated weapons from Russia worth $ 3 billion.

The recent setting up of a consignment warehouse and a service centre in India called Rosoboron Service may go a long way in meeting India's requirements for uninterrupted supply of spare parts and for repair and maintenance of equipment of Russian origin. During Prime Minister Dr. Manmohan Singh's Moscow visit in December 2005, an intellectual property rights agreement in respect of military equipment was signed.

6 Relations with Super Powers : USA, China and Russia

6.1 Relations with USA

Relations with USA were for a long time one sided. India was all admiration for USA for their own struggle for independence and for their sympathy for India's struggle for independence. American regard for all human beings as equal and their disregard for feudal old world order was an inspiration. India was fully with the USA in the organization of the UN. The United States, however, saw India as a poor underdeveloped country but with a penchant for high minded posturing not realizing the realities of the world founded then on the victory of the allies in the World War, a victory in which India could share only what was allotted to her by the Western powers guided by UK. The Western powers were led by Churchill in opposition to the Soviet Union. The Soviet Union also was raring to spread communism and Russian hegemony in Europe and later in the whole world. India's opposition to military alliances and the US attitude of treating India and Pakistan as equals regarding the Kashmir problem under reference to UN increased the distance between USA and India. There were hopes that the administration of John F. Kennedy would have more sympathy for Indian policy, but India was soon disappointed. India recognized the Fidel Castro regime in Cuba and did not toe the line of the United States in the Cuban missile crisis. India was one of the leaders and founders of the Non-aligned movement among the Third World countries which was frowned upon by USA as not salutary to the interest of the Western powers.

Some Americans dubbed India as a fellow traveller when India pleaded for universal disarmament. Some change of attitude occurred after President Eisenhower's visit to India. The President noticed how the Indian public exerted to show their welcome and appreciation for USA as a humane nation whose values of philanthropy and democracy touched their hearts. As a result of this visit USA increased their economic and food assistance to India. More educational and cultural exchanges also emerged. When Mrs. Indira Gandhi was the Prime Minister, India took the decision not to sign the NPT which they felt was partial to the atom bomb holding countries. India was also critical about USA assisting France to continue to rule over Vietnam. USA reacted to Indian decisions by refusing the supply of nuclear fuel for its legitimate needs.

During the latter part of the 1960s, India took interest in the international economic cooperation and became a founder member of the UNCTAD and the group of 77. India actively worked for the conferences on the Law of the Sea and discussions concerning space exploration. India assisted the UN wholeheartedly in peace keeping operations in the Congo, the Gaza strip, Cypress and Lebanon. These activities raised India's stock with the USA. About two years after the liberation of Bangladesh and quick Indian withdrawal from there, Indo-US relations became warmer. They signed an agreement in 1974 to strengthen their bilateral ties. India because of her commitment to non-alignment refused to join the Asian Security Plan advanced by the Soviet Union. India also desired to normalize her relations with the super power China, the next door neighbour.

An important landmark of 1974 for India was the successful nuclear implosion experiment by Indian scientists at Pokhran. This was done as an Indian response to the clandestine nuclear programme of Pakistan under instructions of their Prime Minister Mr. Z.A. Bhutto with the help of China. After the Pokhran implosion, tremendous international pressure was exerted on India to go slow in the nuclear programme. Only in 1998, after a gap of twenty-four years India had as a follow up series of successful nuclear experiments. Pakistan also carried out similar experiments. India suffered now sanctions against her from nuclear powers for proceeding with atom bomb development. In 1977, Mr. Morarji Desai became the Prime Minister heading the Janata Party. He was assured by President Carter that USA could resume fuel supplies to Tarapore if India desisted from development of atomic weapons or reprocessing of spent fuel. The stalemate continued. The USA, it seems, was also responsible for blocking the $5.8 billion aid from the International Monetary Fund. Mrs. Gandhi reached an understanding with President Ronald Reagen which resulted in his agreeing to let France supply the nuclear fuel for the Tarapore plant under the safeguards agreed to by Mrs. Gandhi for that reactor. India and USA signed fresh agreements during Mrs. Gandhi's official visit to Washington D.C. in 1982.

Rajiv Gandhi was sworn in as Prime Minister of India after his mother's assassination in 1984. Rajiv Gandhi was instrumental in convening a six-nation conference on disarmament along with Sweden and Mexico. He presented an action plan for a nuclear free, non-violent world order. India's economic growth had crossed annual increase of 9 per cent. India is now an attractive destination for foreign investments. According to the projections of Goldman Sachs of New York, by 2050 Indian GDP would cross $ 28,000 billion. India, South Africa and Brazil joined together to focus on alleviation of hunger and poverty. They issued a joint statement of the three multi-racial and multi-cultural democracies indicating their intention to follow a policy of maximum good of most of their citizens by conducting their foreign relations strictly on moral standards.

The terrorist attack on US Trade Towers in New York brought home to the US, the suffering India had endured due to terrorism from terrorist sanctuaries in Pakistan and Pakistan occupied Kashmir. The USA now sought alliance with Pakistan and also India against world-wide threat of terrorism particularly active in multi-religious countries with pockets of Muslims like Russia, India or China. The secularist and peaceful policies of India prevailed on USA to seek rapprochement between India and Pakistan. Both USA and India had not appreciated the violent emergence of Pakistan trained Taliban in Afghanistan. Under pressure of USA, Pakistan has apparently distanced herself from the Taliban especially because they after their eviction from Afghanistan have targeted Pakistan for creating a base for themselves. An important step in India-US cooperation was initiated by the mutual understanding that India and USA will try to collaborate in developing nuclear energy for civilian purposes even when India's objections to the NPT remain unresolved. The hurdles in finalizing the welcome measure is US practice of applying its own laws in detail to mutually acceptable projects.

6.2 Marked Improvement in Relations

There has been marked improvement in the Indo-US relations since the second term of the Bill Clinton administration. President George W. Bush has been pushing the US relations with India to a new high. The Indian Government of Atal Behari Vajpayee characterized the United States as India's natural ally. When the United Progressive Alliance (UPA) government took over in India in May 2004, the Prime Minister Dr. Manmohan Singh gave the highest priority to the improvement of relations with United States. The Bush administration too counted the improvement as an achievement of their foreign policy. The then designated Secretary of State Ms. Condoleezza Rice said in the Foreign Relations Committee that the USA was cooperating with India, the world's largest democracy across a range of economic and security issues.

India and the US established a joint working group on counter terrorism in January 2000. After the September 11, 2001 terrorist attack on the US, the strategic relationship gathered momentum. According to the former Deputy Secretary of State Strobe Talbott, the campaign on behalf of freedom, liberty and democracy and the war on terrorism would go a long way to define what might be a common agenda between the United States and India. India backed the US led war against Al Qaeda and the Taliban in Afghanistan. India and the US entered into agreements to counter terrorist threats. The US included some terrorist organizations operating from Pakistan in their list of terrorist groups. Dawood Ibrahim was declared as a global terrorist. General Musharraf promised not to allow Pakistan territory to be used by the terrorist organizations, but the terrorist training camps continued to exist in Pakistan. Only after the murder of Ms. Bhutto the new government of Pakistan has open hostility for the terrorist organizations entrenched in Pakistan.

India and the US have begun joint military exercises and naval ship calls. The educational and training programmes, exchange operational procedures and mutual visits of high civil and military officials are occurring. In January 2004, Prime Minister Atal Behari Vajpai signed an agreement on the next step in strategic partnership, which included missile defence, cooperation in civilian nuclear and space programmes and in high technology trade. The defence related sales to India jumped to $ 900 million by 2004. The US has been India's topmost trading partner. In 1990, the bilateral trade was $ 5.6 billion. In 2003 it rose to $ 18.3 billion. A favourable trade balance for India has been increasing. The contentious issues in trade relations like high tariff, intellectual property rights and market access are being attended to. The US has been one of the largest FDI investors in India. In portfolio investment also in India, US is a leading investor. India too has been making direct investments in the US. India has signed the New Framework for US-India defence relations for ten years in order to maintain security and stability and to protect free flow of commerce. In this framework, a Defence Production Group was set up in order to oversee the trade in defence items. The Defence Minister, Pranab Mukherjee has also stated that the Government of India remains steadfast in its independent foreign policy. The cooperation would always be in mutual interest.

After the July 2005 meeting between Dr. Manmohan Singh and President George W. Bush, a joint statement declared that the two countries were keen to transform their relationship into global partnership. They expressed their intent to expand cooperation in space, civilian uses of atomic energy and the dual use of technology. Dr. Manmohan Singh was assured that the President of the US would work to achieve full cooperation with India in the civilian uses of nuclear energy and related trade including expeditious supply of fuel to safeguard nuclear reactors at Tarapore, but not limited to it. The US has been emphasizing on the separation plan requiring India to move 14 of its 22 nuclear reactors under permanent international safeguards by the year 2014 and place all future civilian reactors under same safeguards. Turning to South East Asia, attention was focused on India-Pakistan relations. Dr. Manmohan Singh said that India sincerely believed that a strong, stable, prosperous and moderate Pakistan was in the interest of India.

The US views defence cooperation with India in the context of common principles and shared national interests such as combating terrorism, preventing weapons proliferation and for maintaining stability. The issue of arms sale to India was an important one. In 2002, the Pentagon had negotiated a sale to India of 12 radar sets worth $ 190 million. And India had purchased $ 29 million worth of counter-terrorism equipment for its special forces and had also received sophisticated electronic ground sensors against infiltration of terrorists in Kashmir. The US State Department also authorized Israel to sell to India the jointly developed Falcon air-borne early warning system. The Bush administration had expressed reservations about Indian negotiations in Iran and Pakistan for a gas pipeline for supply of Iranian gas, but India has, under the compulsion of energy shortage and friendly relations with both Iran and Pakistan, gone ahead with the gas pipeline project which is still in the planning stage along with a northern supply pipeline across Afghanistan and Pakistan. India has been in the midst of a major and rapid economic expansion. Despite various problems, the current growth rate in Indian economy is quite high. It is likely to go much higher in the near future. The economic relations have been the backbone of the rapidly advancing strategic relationship between India and the United States. India and the US account for about 27 per cent of world production.

6.3 Nuclear Trade

The United States Senate Foreign Relations Committee approved a bill in June 2006 to amend US laws in order to permit nuclear trade with India which is not a signatory to the nuclear Non Proliferation Treaty. Senator John Kerry said that such a deal would be most sensible. Unlike other NPT signatories, India has been a good steward of nuclear materials and technologies. A related bill was passed in the House of International Relations Committee. The bill required an annual Presidential certification that India has met its commitments under the July 2005 joint statement, its operation plan, India's safeguards agreement and additional protocol with the IAEA, the 123 agreement and the US applicable laws regarding US exports to India. The deal will ensure immediate supply of uranium to India's existing nuclear power plants. India will be able to increase its power supply to 20,000 MW by 2020. The deal will open techno-commercial activity worth at least 100 billion dollars with the members of the nuclear supplier group. India would be accepted a *de facto* nuclear weapons state outside the NPT. India has declared a voluntary moratorium on further tests concerning development of nuclear weapons. The left parties objection in India was primarily doctrinaire being afraid that the deal will strengthen capitalist and imperialist USA. According to Dr. Abdul Kalam, the former President of India, the deal should be pursued to success since we have low reserves of uranium and considerable effort and time are still required for developing thorium based reactors. India is now on the way to operationalise the deal which is practically now a national commitment to the leadership displayed by the Congress. The left has withdrawn their support which they were extending to the United Progressive

Alliance government at the Centre, but other groups rallied to the leadership displayed by the Congress. There is wide international support visible to this deal which brings solace to the lovers of reasoned growth of world peace and prosperity.

6.4 India-China Relations

We begin by quoting from Nanda's (1997) book on *India's Policy of Coexistence* :"India was proud of China's struggle against imperialism and sympathized with it on the Japanese onslaught which weakened it so much that Chiang's national army could not withstand the communist uprising." At the end of the World War, the communists were in control and Chiang took shelter in Taiwan with security provided by the US navy. China has secured Hong Kong and Macao, but Taiwan is holding out, having become a foothold in Asia culturally and politically of USA. China has extended its administration by force to the autonomous Tibet region of China. The Dalai Lama who was the religious and political head of Tibetans fled to India in 1959 followed by many influential Tibetans. The Dalai Lama has a large following in India too. In granting asylum to the fugitive Tibetans, India treated them as innocent neighbours in deep trouble. The Dalai Lama was allowed to set up his camp near Dalhousie in the Himalayan foothills with the understanding that he would return to Tibet when he can do so voluntarily. Dalai Lama had no record of rebellion against the suzerainty of China. India has also conveyed to China that the Tibetan refugees would love to return to Tibet and the Dalai Lama should be allowed to discuss this return with them implying some modicum of autonomy to the Tibetans in the Tibet region of China. The negotiations were marred by recent violent confrontations in Lhasa. The Dalai Lama has appealed to the Tibetans to shun violence and has offered to negotiate afresh. India is also keen to have an amicable settlement and also an end to the unsettled border between China including the Tibet region and India. India is hopeful of redefining the international boundary on the *Panchsheel* principles agreed to by both the countries. Due consideration has to be given to the traditional as well as geographic considerations.

Of late China and India are having many exchanges to promote trade and scientific research. The Pakistan-China highway across the Kashmir territory now under adverse control of Pakistan has been assured of stability and protection when India regains control of this territory. The international climate of business has also improved. The MNC's are increasingly visible in all countries. Both China and India are dismantling controls imposed over production and marketing.

As stated earlier, Indian policy of co-existence has been formalized in *Panchsheel* enunciated in the agreement on trade and intercourse between the Tibet region of China and India on 29th April, 1954, based on mutual respect for each other's territorial integrity. *Panchsheel* was incorporated into ten principles of international peace and cooperation in the Bandung Conference. On 11th December, 1957, the UN General Assembly unanimously adopted the resolution on peaceful co-existence presented by India, Yugoslavia and Sweden. The non-aligned conference in1961 accepted *Panchsheel* as the core of the movement. Premier Chou-en Lai assured Nehru that China will not be averse to accepting McMahon line as *de facto* frontier. The Chinese later laid claim to about 40,000 sq. miles of Indian territory. As a result of escalation of border patrolling and border clashes, the Chinese decided to launch a full scale attack on India in 1962, but on finding that India had no aggressive designs on China, they declared a unilateral cease-fire and withdrew to the established borders. As a corollary China and Pakistan developed strategic links and India and Russia became close friends. India now concentrated on defence preparedness and industrialization. India soon reached the level of advanced countries in many new technologies and in nuclear energy production. India strengthened its ties with the developing world. Both India and China are hopeful that they would reach a border agreement in the near future. The tension from controversial maps and continued reiteration of claims will subside only when the agreement is signed and made public. The threat of fundamentalism visible in corners of both India and China as well as in Russia and USA, is bringing the policies of all threatened states in line. Nepal has emerged out of feudal order and is now become a parliamentary democracy. India is still beset with Maoist insurrection in Bihar or the tribal clashes in some of the North East Indian states. China because of wisdom gained through centuries of wars and rebellions will deal with India more correctly once India appears to them to have overcome unrest in some states and the niche occupied by the communists in Indian democracy continues to be stable. China is supporting the Indo-American nuclear deal so far.

A Joint Working Group at the level of Vice Ministers for strengthening peace and tranquillity along the boundary was formed. Three agreements as confidence building measures on cooperation in science and technology, civil aviation, and cultural exchanges were concluded. Another Joint Working Group was set up to promote trade and investment relations. Discussions were held with the President Deng Xiaoping and other top leaders, in which the Chinese stressed the need for promoting the social and economic development in the two countries and for safeguarding regional and global peace. The modification, to satisfy both sides, of the line of control is also being discussed.

6.5. A Turn Around in India-China Relations

Following the nuclear tests conducted by India in May 1998, some chill descended on the India-China relations. During the visit of Prime Minister Atal Behari Vajpayi to China in 2003, purposeful negotiations were begun between the two countries regarding the boundary dispute and economic cooperation. The dramatic expansion of bilateral trade in recent years has provided a stabilizing factor. The export of iron ore to China has been expanding. China's entry into the World Trade Organization has huge investment potential. By 2010 India-China trade is likely to touch $ 60 billion. As per the Chinese Ambassador to India, there are over 50 Chinese companies involved in many infrastructure projects in India like power, highways, telecommunications etc. More than 150 companies from India are active in various projects in China. The year 2006 has been celebrated as "Year of Friendship, Culture and Cooperation" in both the countries.

Prime Minister Dr. Manmohan Singh visited China in 2008. A joint statement issued at the end of the visit said that the two countries were firmly committed to resolve their outstanding differences through peaceful negotiations. The two sides welcomed the successful completion of their first joint military training exercise held at Kunming in China in December 2007. They have agreed to hold the next joint exercise in India. The Prime Minister's visit was significant. The two powerful nations have moved closer. Besides a positive pledge to cooperate in the civil use of nuclear energy, China is seen to be supportive of Indian aspirations in the UN and the UN Security Council. Dr. Manmohan Singh assured China that India will not join any alliance for containing China. The PM said that the sustained growth of China and India was practically a public good at this time when uncertainty gripped the world economy amid fears of recession in USA and Japan. Mrs. Sonia Gandhi, the Chairperson of the ruling UPA in India had also visited China before the PM's visit. Leaders from both sides affirmed that the relations between China and India are not just bilateral ties but an assurance of world peace. Eleven agreements were signed during the visit of the PM covering wide spectrum from economic planning, housing, health and culture. In an address delivered in Beijing, the PM said that we will pursue our objectives in the Asian way avoiding confrontation and building trust, confidence and consensus. India and China have an important role to play in the building of world peace, security and regional stability.

6.6 International Cooperation

India and Pakistan are both allies of USA in its fight against terrorism. USA and India have been major targets of Islamic *jehad* operating from sanctuaries in Pakistan under control of the Taliban, Al Qaeda and other extremist organisations like Lashkar-e-Tayyeba and Jamat taking orders from their leaders. Pakistan had a hand in nourishing Taliban as Islamic agitational tool against India for prying out the Indian Kashmir from secular India and USA kept arming Pakistan who was diverting military equipment to its Taliban cadres. But after the Taliban became more ambitious and started aiming at subverting the Pakistan state, the elected government of Pakistan has boldly announced their military offensive against the Taliban strongholds in Pakistan. USA and India can now expect more cooperation from Pakistan. The peace talks between the new Pakistan President and Dr. Manmohan Singh, the present Indian Prime Minister have restarted after break in protest at Pakistan not doing enough to thwart terrorism from its soil against India. Pakistan is very cautious because of unrest in its various parts, and the continuing suspicion of India in spite of settled policy of India to win over Pakistan's friendship. The new government of Pakistan has only to fulfil its pledges against terrorism.

There was a detente in the cold war after an understanding was reached between President Reagen of USA and Gorbachev, head of the Soviet Union after the Soviet Union backed off in a star war challenge. Gorbachev had become fascinated by the rate of development of the non-communist world. He decided to democratize the communist system and to liberalize the economy. The Taliban who had been encouraged by the West to liberate Afghanistan from the communist factions now began to spread their version of Islamic power in Afghanistan and the people there again rebelled. The civil war is still continuing. The Afghan nationalists hold Kabul in alliance with the USA and many friends of Afghanistan including India, while the Taliban are strong in the south. India has developed helpful links regarding education, communication and health with the government of Afghanistan. The USA is aware of Pakistan's support to Taliban aggression in Afghanistan and giving verbal support to USA aganist them.

The Delhi declaration of Rajiv and Gorbachev on November 27, 1986 was a landmark that emphasized abjuring of violence and intimidation, inequality, oppression and discrimination. They stressed the need for rechannelising the resources from armaments to social and economic development. Both leaders called for destruction of nuclear arsenals and barring of all weapons from outer space. Cooperation between India and the Soviet Union reached a high level. Unfortunately the Soviet Union was not prepared yet for Gorbachev's revolution and it disintegrated from the yoke of central direction.

6.7 Indian View

Indian ambitions are non-hegemonic. She does not wish to be a pole, believing firmly that all problems can be solved by discussion and mutual accommodation. India, South Africa and Brazil showed a new direction in international relations by forming IBSA with a focus on the alleviation of hunger and poverty, ensuring sustainable development and expanding trade among the three countries. A joint statement was issued affirming that the three countries would be moulding their foreign policy in the light of their discussions following strictly moral standards. The common view of India is that all probems can be solved by mutual discussion and goodwill.

Russia has emerged as a leading supplier of energy and India is one of the fastest growing markets for energy. Another sector of great potential is small and medium enterprises. The Russian Public Organization for these sectors has concluded an MOU with the federation of Indian Chambers of Commerce to explore common development facilities. Cooperation can span training, exchange of experts, supply of machinery and equipment. There can be contracts for turnkey execution of projects. India supported Russian accession to the WTO. Economic partnership provides a secure underpinning of their decades long friendship. Russia and India confirmed of their adherence to the common ideals of secularism, democracy, rule of law, cultural diversity and co-existence. President

Putin stressed "India is a crucial factor of stability in the region and in the world as a whole. Russia would like to see India play an important role in the international affairs. In October 2000, Vladimir Putin, successor to President Yeltsin and the Indian Prime Minister agreed to develop the strategic partnership into one befitting the expected multi-polar world order. They also saw the relevance of bipolar cooperation between the three nations: Russia, China and India, at normal pace. Both desired to strengthen the UN. There was much scope for mutual cooperation in energy and industry sectors. India and Russia would also strengthen the WTO.

Comrade Putin has vigorousy held that India's membership of the UN Security Council should be with the right of veto. Putin also evinced his interest in collaboration with India in civilian nuclear energy. Russia under President Medwedev had promised to give perpetual supply of nuclear fuel unconditionally to the nuclear power plants Kundankulam in Tamil Nadu. In the past India received great help from the Soviet Union and friendship with is a continuation of that understanding. During the first visit of President Putin to India, deals for the supply of equipment worth $ 3 billion were made that included the supply of Airborne warning and control systems, submarines, and missiles. The aircraft carrier Gorshkov will also be delivered to India in the near future.

The recent setting up of a consignment warehouse and a service centre in India will go a long way for an uninterrupted supply of spare parts as well as maintenance of equipments of Russian origin. Joint production projects are also envisaged, *e.g.*, for supersonic cruise missile. India-Russia trade is likely to triple by 2010.

Prime Minister Dr. Manmohan Singh's visit to Russia in 2009 has further strengthened relations between the two countries. Both president Medvedev and Prime Minister Dr. Manmohan Singh have reiterated Russia's support to India in various spheres including the fight against terrorism and in the sphere of nuclear cooperation.

7 Relations with Neighbours

7.1 Introduction

India's relations with the Muslim countries in the west amounted to immigration of adventurers, travellers and seekers of fortune in India, usually with the trading caravans and now and then as armed bands. West Asia provided the hinterland for expansionist Muslim armies operating in India from Lahore or Delhi as forward outposts. Arab Caliph had secured Sind by a military expedition very early but further inroads were blocked and the Arabs were bound by treaty not to attack any other Indian kingdoms. The Vijaynagar empire of South India and the rulers of Andhra had direct communications with the countries of the East. The Delhi Sultans attended to the security of India by establishing armed contingents along the borders and erecting new defensive forts in Delhi and Sialkot. There was closer relationship of Mughal India with Iran who had helped the fleeing Humayun to retake Delhi. Akbar invited Iranian artists to stay in his court and got many Indian artists trained in illuminating manuscripts. The growth of the Mughal miniature painting was followed by Jaipur and Pahari paintings. Carpet weaving became a speciality of Kashmir under the tutelage of master craftsmen of Iran. The Arabs transmitted Indian philosophy, science and technology to the West. Sufis and Muslim preachers and traders from Gujarat propagated Islam in the Maldives, Sri Lanka and Malaysia. With the decline of the Mughal empire and with the passing of Indian trade into British East India Company's control reduced Indian (Hindu and Muslim) contacts with the neighbouring countries. Earlier, Indian kingdoms of the Deccan, Manipur, Maharashtra, the Khalsa empire of Ranjit Singh made some ripples of curiosity in the world where Europeans had started fresh empire building from Napoleon's times. India did not yet possess a national perspective and only thought in terms of religious or provincial identity. The Muslim rulers of Delhi wished to protect their Indian holdings against possible encroachments of other Indian rulers or from Mughals from beyond Afghanistan. When Mughals ruled at Delhi, they strengthened their borders which included Afghanistan. Aurangzeb had begun to think of India as a nation so long as the Mughal dynasty continued to preside at Delhi. The Marathas too wanted the Great Mughal to continue to reign allowing them to rule. Only Tipu Sultan of Mysore attempted to secure military alliance with the French or the Portuguese. When the British became masters of Delhi, they worked hard to secure internal order and external security of their possession of India. India was projected as a burden for the British which they were opening up to Christianity and European superior civilization. The British nourished independent states as buffers with expanding Czarist Russia or China. Afghanistan and the Tibet region of China were strengthened as buffer states. Europe was monitored by encroaching over the independence of Egypt and building strong British position at Aden and at Singapore. Indians hardly had any say when the British Indian army waged imperialist wars in Africa or opium wars in China. A lucrative profession for the young soldiers from the Punjab was to be enrolled in Shanghai police or the Hong Kong contingent.

The Indian princes were caged with pensions in their rump states earning British honours from the scale of their service to strengthen the British Empire. They kept practically half of India satisfied under *status quo* of penury and superstition. The British still acted as change agents in the major half of the country ruled and administered by them. The intellectuals there created a renaissance of Indian culture and a consciousness of loss of freedom.

The princes sent their secret agents to Russia or any up and coming European power for aid in ridding India of the British but to no avail. With the success of Russian revolution led by Lenin, the intellectuals from Punjab especially Muslims flocked to Tashkent seeking financial and military aid for a revolution in India. Victory in the Great War strengthened the British and their allies or Russia still further. The Indian nationalists now found consolation in the leadership of Mahatma Gandhi who gave them hope of emancipation using modern tools of agitation and boycott, together with age-old non-cooperation and non-violence. The impatient among the nationalists like Netaji Subhas Chandra Bose hoped to achieve Indian independence through the attack of the fascist powers on the British empire. The victory of the allies and freedom of India are recent events. Free India is out to build afresh friendly relations with all countries whatever be their past situation. As a parting legacy, the British managed to create sectional leaders in India who managed to help them partition the country and the nationalists accepted partition against the threat of Balkanization. Pakistan was created out of India. In place of India having two votes in international parleys, the Imperialists created a negative vote of Pakistan often against Indian perceptions. After almost a century of further tribulations and strenuous efforts, India seems to have managed to gain the confidence of the present leaders of great powers and of Pakistan and can look forward to global progress with a glorious role for all nations, big and small. Poverty had driven thousands of Indians under semi-slave conditions to many Asian, African and Latin American countries with the connivance of the British in India. Here in this chapter we shall discuss Indian relations with small neighbours.

7.2 Afghanistan

The Second Regional Economic Cooperation Conference on Afghanistan was held in New Delhi on November 18 and 19, 2006. The objective of the Conference was to look into the issues of energy, transport, business and agriculture needs of Afghanistan and to reassure support to the Afghan Government from the international community particularly the regional states. The Conference discussed a range of issues. The meeting included Iran's Minister Manuchehr Mottaki, the French Foreign Minister Philippe Douste Blazy and the Russian Foreign Minister Sergey Lavrov. Some key officials of the US and Pakistan also participated. Another meeting between representatives of the business and industry federations of India and Afghanistan was held to discuss private sector investments. China and aid agencies like the Agha Khan Development Network were also invited to the Conference. Since the Conference was held at Delhi, it implied that Pakistan was reconciled to India playing a relevant role in providing assistance to Afghanistan.

India's Prime Minister, Dr. Manmohan Singh, assured New Delhi's support to the Afghan Government. The admission of Afghanistan to SAARC in 2006 had been an important event. India's efforts to boost trade with Afghanistan have not succeeded fully, though the Zaranj-Delaram highway has been completed and opened formally by Indian Minister, Parnab Mukherji.

The Afghan President Hamid Karzai visited New Delhi from April 9 to April 12, 2006, when many issues were discussed with emphasis on terrorism. The Indian Government pledged additional assistance of $50 million, making the total assistance to $650 million. Another $50 million was given as line of credit. Hamid Karzai had meetings with the representatives of the Federation of Indian Chambers of Commerce and Industry (FICCI) and Confedration of Indian Industries (CII) and had visited Hyderabad. A large number of Indian specialists and technicians have been working in Afghanistan to assist them in rebuilding its damaged economy and institutions. Indo-Tibetan Border Police personnel are deployed for security of Indian workers. Two terrorist suicide attacks have been made on the Indian Embassy at Kabul which caused considerable damage.

The Governments of Afghanistan and India have set up an

India-Afghanistan Foundation for fostering educational, cultural scientific and technical cooperation between the two countries. The foundation has set up a trust fund for financing higher studies of Afghan citizens in institutions of higher learning in India. It also finances visits and exchanges between India and Afghanistan of scholars, journalists and other personnel. It also contributes to the translation of suitable works of Afghan and Indian authors. The thrust areas include science and culture, health and women's studies.

7.3 Sri Lanka

India and Sri Lanka have been linked from pre-historic times. Sri Lanka was separated from India by the colonial government like the separation of the colonial government of Burma in order to govern these territories better. When the British expanded the tea and other cash crops in Sri Lanka, considerable Indian farm labour was recruited and a system of indenture or time-bound slavery started. In 1947 there were large numbers of stateless persons of Indian origin in Sri Lanka. India desired those born in Sri Lanka to be given citizenship rights. Since this would affect parliamentary elections in that country against Lankan nationalist parties, the proposal was not agreed to and the failure aggravated the demand of local Tamils for a separate Tamil state in Sri Lanka. The Tamils of Tamil Nadu in India supported this against the wishes of the Government of India which favoured the establishment of an autonomous state for Tamils in the north and east within Sri Lanka. The Prime Minister of India, Rajiv Gandhi got the moderate Tamils in Sri Lanka to favour this solution, but there was no agreement forthcoming between the Sri Lanka Government and the LTTE, the liberation army of Tamils. The autonomy proposals initiated by Rajiv Gandhi had broad support of all and were on the verge of successful adoption when on the requirement of surrender of arms by the LTTE, the fighting restarted. India sent an expeditionary force to Sri Lanka to disarm the LTTE without gauging the depth of the separatist preparedness for a civil war. The Indian contingent had to be withdrawn and the problem of an agreed solution to the partition demand had yet to be found. The LTTE imagined that India perhaps was being tough only because of the loyalty to their Prime Minister's involvement in Sri Lankan diplomacy The problem of citizenship or repatriation of stateless persons of Indian origin has been amicably solved with the grant of citizenship to the bulk of Indian immigrants before a certain cut-off date. A fierce civil war raged in Sri Lanka as a result of which the LTTE force capitulated and its supremo, Prabhakaran met his tragic end on May 19, 2009. The war is over, but the problem of a very large number of Tamil refugees is gnawing at the heart of the Sri Lankan authorities. It is one of the most serious problems, this part of the world is confronted with. India has cordial relations with Sri Lanka. India and Sri Lanka both are on world heritage tourist circuit because of the Buddhist monuments in both countries. Sri Lanka's east and west coasts are physically extensions of Indian coasts. The broken land link across Rameswaram in India is ancient evidence of the two countries' togetherness. Sri Lanka is the biggest tea exporter. It has large export trade in spices, tea, rubber, ebony, sandal wood and precious stones. With the development of globalization and removal of trade and travel barriers, coordination between the industries and trade of the two countries can be beneficial to both.

When the Sri Lankan President Jayawardane launched the military campaign against Jaffna in 1987 and ordered a blockade, it had caused panic in the Tamil population in India. This country had to drop air supplies of food to the beleaguered population. Rajiv Gandhi's priority was to ensure that there was no cause of unrest in the Indian state of Tamil Nadu and there was a negotiated settlement. A settlement was worked out on the basis of an autonomous Tamil Ealam within Sri Lanka and the LTTE to surrender their arms. In spite of an Indian Peace Keeping Force sent to aid Sri Lanka in disarming the rebels, the LTTE refused to surrender their arms and reneged from the earlier peace settlement.

The Indian force was withdrawn, the rebellion and counter-action of continued. Rajiv was assassinated by LTTE agent and the negotiations for a fresh settlement on the basis of a smaller autonomous region was being pursued under mediation of Norway. On November 30, 2006, the Prime Minister, Dr. Manmohan Singh and Sri Lankan President agreed to the devolution package evolved by the All Party Representative Committee. India reiterated its earlier stand for a negotiated settlement satisfying all sections of Sri Lankan society. The European Union had banned any dealings with the LTTE. Later the Sri Lankan army stormed the LTTE positions and decimated its leadership.

7.4 Maldives and Laccadives

Laccadives are a small group of islands off the Kerala coast and are part of Indian territory. The islanders converted to Islam through the efforts of preachers from Gujarat. The spoken language in the Laccadives is Urdu and their livelihood depends on fishing bonito and tuna and what else the sea can offer. They also join up as sailors. Laccadives provide Muslim preachers and teachers to Sri Lankan Muslims. The Muslims in Sri Lanka and in Maldives have neighbourly contacts with those of Laccadives.

Maldives is an independent group of Islands off the western coast of Sri Lanka. The Government of Maldives has close and friendly relations with the Government of India. An attempt by pirates and disgruntled elements to secure Maldives as base for their unlawful activities, was thwarted by timely action of the Indian navy. Maldives (airport Male) is a favourite destination of European tourists. It provides viewing of the hidden reef teeming with sea life, and the Sri Lankan cuisine is very popular with them. A single island is allotted to a single hotel and its facilities, another island is for the airport, and similarly different islands are used for different purposes. Maldives (archipelago) is still in the bicycle age; metalled roads do not exist. The people speak their own language (Divehi) allied to Arabic. The main industry is fishing or enlistment with merchant men. Maldives group of islands, is an isolated outpost of human civilization in the middle of the ocean and constitutes a rest spot for fishermen from distant lands. The islands have clear lagoons with white sand beaches. The population is Sunni Muslim. Barrier reefs around 12 atolls supporting 2000 small islands constitute the Maldives archipelago. Most of the islands are too small and uninhabited.

Maldives became free from being a British protectorate in 1965 and became a republic in 1968. Its main export is fish to Sri Lanka. They have two rainy seasons, the home industry is around cowrie shell articles, reed mats and lacquer ware. In 1950, there was a dispute of the nationalists with UK regarding the lease of Gan island for British defence in the Indian ocean. The dispute was settled by Britain abandoning plans to extend its naval outposts to far off places.

7.5 Tibet Region of China

Tibet, a vast tract in the south of China lies to the north of India and shares the Himalayan ranges with India. China when strong ruled over Tibet with a governor residing there. Tibet sometimes asserted its independence and expelled the Chinese representative. Tibet for a couple of centuries ruled over western parts of China extending up to Mongolia. The British rulers of India in the days of the colonial empire practically regarded Tibet as an independent country and tried to keep up also the fiction of Chinese suzerainty. They in their maps kept a strip of land, known as Kafiristan and acknowledged as belonging to Afghanistan between India and China. Colonial India negotiated trade and cultural relations directly with the Tibetan authorities. They also assisted Tibet in the matter of postal services and had Indian police posts on the Tibetan border. There was an agreed border as a part of the McMahon Line demarcating India from Tibet and China. The agreement was not countersigned by the Chinese agent or ratified by China. On India gaining independence and realizing the injustice of these realities, India disbanded any extra-territorial concessions and services in Tibet and invited China to have a border agreement. India however hoped that China would grant autonomy to Tibet as enjoyed customarily by the Tibetans. India proposed Tibetan autonomy to China in a purely neighbourly way. There is a vast following of the Dalai Lama, the god-king of Tibet and the head of Tibeten Lamaism. His followers exist in many countries including Mongolia, India, Nepal and Bhutan. China, on the other hand, had become one of the victorious allies of the World War and regarded such advice as interference. China pushed its communications and exercise of authority in Tibetan part of its territory, so much so that the Dalai Lama had to seek asylum with his government in exile in India. India allowed him to settle at Dharamsala close to the Tibetan border amidst Indian Buddhists already in that region. The Tibetans in exile have prospered and run the affairs of Dalai Lama's followers all over the world though they pine for their autonomous homeland of Tibet. The matter is in the lap of the United Nations. Dalai Lama's prestige as a democratic head of a religion is almost that of the Pope among Christians. India and the Dalai Lama still hope that a formula can be devised through which Tibetans in exile can go back to their homes in Tibet where China is claiming to have carried out modern developments and re-education of the people into the merits of real democracy practiced now in China. China misunderstood India's support of Tibet's autonomy so much so that it attacked India in response to border skirmishes on account of two armies actively patrolling the common border in an atmosphere of persisting claims to pockets across the border under adverse possession. Both China and India now claim that peaceful negotiations will succeed and the defined border will come into force. China is, however, silent on the issue of autonomy of Tibet or the position of the Dalai Lama if he is restored to Lhasa from where his government was forced into exile. There are about 150,000 Tibetan refugees in India.

In the first part of 2009 there were widespread demonstrations by Tibetans all over the world, especially in Tibet and some parts of India. The occasion was provided by the passage of olympic torch to China. Violent action was let loose in Lhasa by the Chinese authorities to stem the force of these demonstrations triggering a wave of sympathy for the case of Tibet's autonomy being suppressed by the Beijing Government.

7. 6. Nepal

The great majority of Nepalese are Hindus and India is their holy land. Nepal has the living Hindu tradition of no distinction between the Hindus and the Buddhists. Nepal and India had an open border with large amount of trade across natural hurdles. The trade was limited to man-loads in general. Many Nepalese were recruited in the British Indian army. Many Hindus and Buddhists go to pilgrim spots in Nepal. Many Nepalese have settled in Bengal and Assam. Some Gorkhas are agitating for a separate state of "Gorkhaland" where the immigrant Nepalese are in majority. It is being viewed by many people as an unnecessary irritation and threat to India's integrity. There is already a move to restrict the free movement of the Nepalese into India. The Nepalese language is related to Hindi. The Sherpas, the hardy mountaineers serving as guides or porters to all Himalayan expeditions, are Nepalese. The Nepalese made excellent soldiers in the British Indian armies especially the Gurungs. Stories of man-beast or the abominable snowman in higher Himalayas exist. The Kingdom of Nepal was consolidated in 1775. Nepal wars started with Gorkha troops attacking East India Company outposts along the Nepal border. These wars cost Nepal about half of the kingdom which was ceded to the East India Company. A dynasty of Ranas providing hereditary Prime Ministers to the King and ruled in his name from1846 to 1951 when the power was restored to King Tribhuvan of the royal dynasty. In 1962 the King inaugurated *Panchayat* democracy keeping real power with the King in line with diarchy established in 1919 in India.

There was a movement in Nepal to have parliamentary democracy with the king becoming a constitutional monarch. Due to tardy progress in the abdication of powers by the King, a civil war like situation developed with Maoists who had hold over the peasants. The Chinese stayed aloof while India was active in trying to bring around the King to pursue parliamentary democracy. Under pressure from the Maoists, the elections yielded rebellious majority that hurled the King from the throne to become a commoner. The veteran parliamentarian G.P. Koirala who became the Prime Minister was soon forced to resign paving the way for the communist Parchanda to take the reigns of government. Now Mr. Nepal has resigned as the Prime Minister and the situation is rather fluid.

The Chinese have now a rail reaching up to Nepal. India has also built border roads to Nepal and is keeping close watch on further happenings there. India is cautious about illegal traffic of arms and drugs into India from Nepal. Many Nepalese seek seasonal employment in India. The casinos in Nepal are an attraction for tourists from abroad. The Nepalese trade imported goods from China and they sent this sometimes overseas. India has given free passage to Nepal for export trade through Kolkata.

7.7 Bhutan

Bhutan is a land-locked country in the north east of India. The kingdom of Bhutan is peopled by followers of the Dalai Lama and are Buddhists. They live in isolated valleys. Thimpu, the capital, has about 10,000 population. Dzongs or fortified monasteries are spread about. The chief Dzong separated from Tibet in 1600 A.D. Wangchuk was declared King in 1907. The British were fully in control. India is very protective about Bhutan and is the only country with an embassy in Thimpu. Bhutan is a mineral rich country and uses the expertise available in India in the exploitation of its resources. Recently it has become a constitutional monarchy and has an elected parliament. It was also able to expel some rebellious elements which had intruded into Bhutan as a sanctuary from newly formed north eastern Indian states. India located its Military training teams in 1962 at Ha and Thimpu. The roads inside Bhutan have been built by the Indian Border Roads Organization (Dantak). India and Bhutan have been cooperatively using 2000 MW out of Bhutan's enormous hydro-electric power potential. Soon the utilization will be raised to 10,000 MW. India buys back half of the power for use in this country.

Bhutan has advanced a new concept of development that in place of maximizing the GNP, they should maximize GNH (or Gross National Happiness). Such a goal emphasizes the environmental and cultural possibilities of a country.

The King of Bhutan pushed democratic reforms in Bhutan. A new citizen act was promulgated in 1985. He also favours an identifying national language, Drukpa, the language of the linguistic majority. The non-Bhutanese cannot function as government servants since 1997. There are many immigrants in Bhutan from Nepal and India. The Nepalese labour was invited about a century ago for clearing jungles from the valleys. Indian immigrants are from Mizoram and other North East Indian states to assist in new industrial and hydroelectric projects. Bhutan is a member of ASGI (South Asian Growth Initiative) of Bhutan, Bangladesh, India and Nepal for multi-sectoral technical and economic cooperation.

The King of Bhutan guided Bhutan to become a democracy. India is very happy to have mutually beneficial relations with the new democracy and has announced development of rail traffic into Bhutan and has also increased hydro-electricity production. Bhutan is a member of the United Nations. The young King of Bhutan paid an official visit to India in December 2009 and signed a number of agreements with this country to strengthen relations between India and Bhutan.

7.8 Myanmar

Burma (Myanmar) became part of British Empire in 1800 A.D.

after wars started with the aggressive attacks from much aggrieved Burma. For some time it was administered from Delhi but was separated from the Indian Empire in1937. The Japanese declared Burma to be independent in 1943 after conquering it from the British empire, but the allied forces reoccupied it soon after. Burma celebrates its independence since 1948. In 1962, U Nu set up a revolutionary council after pacification of the country from a communist stir. In the first democratic elections conducted by a military junta in 2000, the BSPP under the leadership of Ms. Aung San Su Ki won but the junta did not loosen their hold on power and the real leader has been held under house arrest. India has openly sided with the rights of Su Ki to form the government. UN is seized of the problem and some advance towards democratic government can be expected. Su Ki won the Nobel Peace Prize a decade back.

Indian relations with Myanmar were cool. But India has to face the ground reality and so started afresh its diplomatic activity with the junta. Myanmar is a member of ASEAN, the regional Association of South East Asia, and India has now a participating observer status in it. A small island that arose in the north east of Andamans a few years ago has not been claimed by India, allowing Myanmar to lay claim to it. Myanmar has much neighbourly association with India. The art and culture, temple construction style and Buddhism hopped from Bengal to Myanmar. The Thai settlers in Myanmar sent settlers into Assam who remained there as Hindus to rule. The new Assam rulers defended Assam from both the Mughals and the British East India Company. Bahadur Shah Zafar, the exiled last Mughal emperor, was buried in Rangoon where he died in captivity. The INA which attacked the British entered India from the east and had its bases in Myanmar and was given spontaneous assistance by the people of Myanmar.

Myanmar is rich in minerals, crude and other natural resources. Myanmar has been exporting timber and minerals from ancient times. A number of Indians who went there as merchants have settled in the cities and add to the national product there as entrepreneurs. Myanmar will provide important links for rail/ road communications between India and China as well as with Malaysia and Thailand. UN is involved in the plan to have fresh free elections in Myanmar which will be welcome to India as well.

7.9 Bangladesh

Bangladesh before its independence was East Pakistan. The partition of India brought it into Pakistan fold because it was a Muslim majority region on the Eastern borders of India. Pakistan, however, had a ready-made army from the partition arrangements between India and Pakistan. Pakistan from the start treated the eastern wing as a burden that they had to carry and treated its citizens as second class to themselves. Pakistan did not make Bengali, the language of the majority a national language.

Mujib-ur-Rehman, the leader of the Awami League even when a student in the USA had secular ideas and could not understand Pakistan's obsession to oppose J& K accession to India. In the first elections in Pakistan, Mujib's Awami League swept the polls. There was a counter revolution in Bangladesh. The first step was the assassination of Mujib on August 15, 1975 and crowning of the murderer of Mujibur Rehman as the military dictator of Bangladesh. The pro-Pakistani elements of the Bangladesh army now wielded power and gave tacit approval to Pakistan secret service ISI and *jehadi* elements to repeat their Hindu minority baiting. More Hindus migrated to India and more Bengladesh elements were driven to India in order to escape extreme poverty. The strife between the border security forces of India and Bangladesh Rifles became persistent and India had to resort to fencing the border at sensitive points to stop illegal immigration into India.

Now a democratically elected government with Sheikh Haseena Wajed is in power unseating the BNP which had usurped the state through violence and rigged elections. Present elections were held under the control of country's judiciary by common consent. The present Bangladesh Government has cordial relations with India. It has already extradited an ULFA rebel of North East India sheltering in Bangladesh and conspiring against India. The expected opening of communications across North East India and Bangladesh and increase in trans-border trade will assist large population of the SAARC region in general and North East India, Bangladesh and Myanmar in particular. Bangladesh will be vigilant against the *jehadi* miscreants having been the first victim of that mentality.

8 Developing India

8.1 Introduction

A resurgent India primarily means its regaining the ancient position of primacy in arts and sciences and that of a nation with a good mercantile culture. A recognized advantage with India is its large middle class which is well educated and motivated. It has a large population of youth well aware of new technologies and their potential to better serve the needs of the people. It has an expanding internal market which can absorb development costs. On the globalization of trade and commerce, foreign direct investments in India have increased by leaps and bounds. India is a large importer of crude and produces petroleum products for internal as well as export market. It is a serious collaborator for erecting pipelines from Iran and from Central Asia to India across Pakistan.

A resurgent India expects more export of experts in the disciplines of physical, mental or spiritual health, and teachers for the learning of languages, arts and crafts. India has an annual output of teachers and professionals that is mind-boggling and they cannot be all absorbed within the country in spite of rapid expansion occurring in public literacy and education. India has largest area for any nation under cultivation. The climate and physical features of the land have favoured great biodiversity. It has an exceptional share of solar energy that can best be harnessed by expansion of farming and forestry. There are all kinds of agricultural research and training establishments. India is in the forefront of foodgrain revolution and is participating vigorously in the expansion of rice harvest. There are indications of breakthrough in the harvesting of all kinds of pulses. India is floating a grain bank for assistance to countries that unfortunately suffer from food shortages. India has established the world's largest plant gene bank. Globalization has found a natural swimmer in India. It has vigorously pursued the nuclear energy treaty with USA in order to be an equal partner in the spread of nuclear energy and collaborate with developed countries to expand nuclear energy for peaceful purposes. Control of trade in nuclear materials and processes is necessary to stop the siphoning off of some material for weapons of aggression by any rogue nation or by criminals. India can offer reactors and processes of original design for the production of nuclear energy. India believes in the certainty of future prosperity of the poor of the world in the wake of general development and global flow of knowledge and capital. Even tribal folk or those living in forest dwellings would have a share in the new drive for a humanist dispensation. India will be an energetic partner with any nation for peace and cooperation. India's proposals for disarmament are far-reaching and certain to be eventually accepted. India is for the revision of the UN constitution and the veto provisions as well as the CTBT and the non-proliferation treaty so that all countries can subscribe to them without reservation. Indian knowledge and experience is available to all friendly countries within the terms agreed to by the developed countries where they have been the primary resource. India has many original contributions in the field of nuclear energy, bio and nano technologies. Even the tribal folk or those living in forests and in marginal border areas would have a share in the new worldwide drive for a humanist dispensation.

8.2 Medical Research

The greatest advances are expected in the worldwide efforts in medical matters. India is the home of herbs and roots, often the source of all pharmacopoeias. India has plenty of forests and sunshine and, therefore, biodiversity which they propose to harness for the alleviation of disease and for human health. The subject of plant biology is of special interest and for opening new careers for talented scholars. India is engaged in the genetic improvement of crops along with the production of plant enzymes useful to industry in many ways. Microsurgical transplants are being attempted for gene modification. India has started production of protection masks and clothing for escaping from industrial and other accidents. War time needs have given a fillip to Indian manufacture of prosthetics, artificial limbs and blood extenders. India is engaged in research in biochemistry and fermentation. Indian graduates and scientists in these areas are in demand in other countries. India is particularly fortunate in the export of its trained medical men and women as well as computerized management skills.

India's long coastline, and century-old interest in coastal fisheries is now reaching the stage of starting deep sea fishing and commercial fishing including fish farming and prawn production for internal consumption as well as for export. There are proposals to introduce refrigerated transport for the dispatch of sea-food within India or abroad. Marine parks are being developed for support of research and training. India is already on the tourist books for medical treatment in new modern hospitals and under the care of best doctors at much lower costs. Purely Indian Ayurvedic treatment also attracts patients from abroad to village doctors of Kerala or fully furnished Ayurvedic hospitals in other parts of the country. Marine biological products and by-products of abattoirs are being processed for special drugs and medicines. In pharmacy research, standardization and purification of drugs have to be tested on large number of volunteers after animal house experiments. This work before marketing drugs is very expensive and time consuming. Since India has conducted such work in their public health programmes, they can carry out such testing for global companies as well. Medical education is relatively inexpensive in India and is very popular. Many teaching hospitals in developed countries are making arrangements for partial medical education in Indian institutions. Indian nurses from the states of Orissa and

Kerala can be seen in hospitals all over the world. Indian voluntary medical teams are often in demand overseas either with Indian peace-keeping contingents or as humanitarian assistance by Indian Red Cross. More medical research teams can function in Indian major hospitals funded by international medical planning. Many newly started medical teaching institutions are receiving donations of costly medical equipment from foreign companies, non-resident Indians and grateful patients. Intense study and research is advancing in biology and bio-technology having basic contribution to the advancement of medical knowledge.

8.3 Disarmament and World Peace

India is fully committed to all necessary steps towards world peace including disarmament, control of weapons and destruction of disproportionate stock of weapons. Thus the concern is particularly about the nuclear weapons and the production of such weapons or their components or wilful spread of underlying designs and special materials and components. India is willing to pursue legitimate trade in drugs, nuclear reactors and atomic energy reactors and instruments for peaceful purposes. India has made certain advances in this area which can be beneficial in the nuclear energy field and for the competitive edge in the efficient use of nuclear materials. India is fully involved in the detection network for atomic explosions, monitoring stations for clandestine production and transportation of dangerous materials and critical components. India presided over the disarmament conference in 2003. This is an evidence of the desire of the international community for curtailing the urge to amass weapons as part of national security. The measures to strengthen international policing and surveillance of hot spots and for increased vigilance are called for. Military contingents seconded for international peace-keeping should be stationed at selected key points regarded as UN sanctuary places which can receive and carry on safe keeping and eventual destruction of surplus weapons from various self-burdened nations.

The USA is reputed to have a stockpile of 15,000 nuclear weapons. Essential stockpiles of weapons should be kept separate from remaining excessive production which deserves destruction under international supervision. India signed the international convention for the suppression of nuclear terrorism in July 2006. If the UN functions in a dispassionate democratic manner, their recommendations to various nations should be pursued to the letter in the interest of justice.The way to solve international problems is through discussions. If the progress of the discussions restricted to parties in confrontation with each other is slow, the UN could assist in accelerating the process. The state of happiness in the world under various heads should be continuously monitored and publicized by a separate UN body. The veto has some advantages for an aggrieved party which may be cornered by false accusations made bold by planned Goebblian propaganda. The veto being exercised by any set of nations howsoever strong, should give place to veto by a separate world peace council set up for the purpose by UN General Assembly every two years, constituted of five chosen individuals of proven wisdom and integrity from all over the world made prominent by their record of service.

The export/import control has to be particularly watchful for erection of mechanical manipulators and acquisition by non-authorized bodies of macro computers. Enumeration and record of all cruise missiles as assembled ready for use or in knocked down state should be filed with the UN appointed disarmament official of the area. Cruise missiles are feared to be deadly for offensive display of power and are marketed in the usual arms trade. In 1982, India proposed a convention on "Stay put" together with a cut off date for the production of fissile materials for weapons. In 1988, Rajiv Gandhi, the Indian Prime Minister presented an action plan with a time-bound framework for 22 years aimed at total elimination of nuclear weapons. Such a programme should, after revising the UN Constitution, be adopted and endorsed by all countries in the interest of stable progress in the world. India has called CTBT as an unequal treaty. Some nations have reservations about the non-proliferation treaty as it now stands and time has already shown its comparative irrelevance. These treaties should be reframed to attract universal acceptance. All nations have to agree to stop further development, refinement and production of missiles.

8.4 Tourism

Tourism can be regarded as a major linking activity between people living all over the world. Tourism has considerable commercial potential and it, along with heritage tourism, is recommended as an earning resource for the UN. China has urged in 2005, the possibility of tourists view of outer space in space capsules launched from a space platform. Other UN income could be from legitimate trade in narcotics and tourism related casinos. UN estates will be established by international law near heritage sites. Nations would be directed to transfer excess of weapons and ammunition including cruise missiles to such sites pending their destruction by experienced staff or final disposal. UN sites would have conference halls, displays and exhibitions. India is planning to afford one tour to a site of choice to every citizen.

8.5 Biotechnology

Advances in biotechnology, genetic modification, stem cell research are the resource for future inventions aiding medicine and longevity. Recent understanding of the RNA will lead to quenching of unwanted activity of specific genes and this will lead to products for combating cancer and HIV. India has contributed to the design of a new bioreactor. There has been progress in the use of plant cells as factories for metabolic products. Genome technology will lead to altered natural fruits and vegetables for consumer preference. Biocatalysts are being developed for useful applications. Intensive research is underway in molecular cell biology, diffusion across membranes, computer simulation of cell division and in the decay of neurons.

European molecular biology organization is enthusiastic about the use of DNA to form electronic components. DNA is the best nanowire; "it is self-assembling, self-reproducing and can adopt various states and conformations." The DNA electronics uses techniques of genetic engineering. They use atomic scale microscopy and optical tweezers to align a single DNA molecule on an electron. DNA can function as a template for deposition of metal atoms allowing certain sites to be protected. DNA has considerable potential as a biological computer component, and can be used as a part of other biomolecular devices that are going to bring about the next technology revolution. This is the time for planning higher education and practical experience in biotechnology. Biotechnology of the future will have new enzymes from protein engineering and cell biology. Plant cells will be used for the accelerated production of natural products. Biocatalysis will require isolated enzymes. Biocatalysis can produce required spatial patterns in polymers.

Much is expected for the understanding of complex diseases through stem cell research. "Stem cells are immature clonogenic self-renewing proginator cells that have the capacity to give rise to mature functioning cells." Stem cells can be derived from the bone marrow or the umbilical cord. Implantable disease corrective deviants are likely to be made with stem cells interfaced on silicon material. The cord blood bank that stores cord blood for twenty-one years for a fee is regarded as providing insurance for the future needs of the body. The embryonic stem cells are capable of developing into any of more than 200 cell types that make the human body. First stem cell transplantation centre has been set up at Chennai for the treatment of leukemia, stroke, diabetes and spinal cord injuries. The All India Institute of Medical Sciences at Delhi is attempting stem cell treatment for heart disease. The Bangalore based Cryostem Karnataka Pvt. Ltd. has a stem cell project for Malaysia Stem Life Corporation. New lines of bioplastics will be designed for special applications concerning transplantation of organs particularly artificial organs engineered genetically.

8.6 Fusion Research

Fusion research is potentially the most promising but extremely expensive. Developed nations are already spending considerable amount on it. If successful, this will open up almost unlimited energy prospects in the service of humanity. The research will involve more than one pathway to be explored. When two atoms are compelled in the appropriate apparatus to fuse their nuclei together, there is some tiny fraction of combined mass converted into energy. The proportionality factor between lost mass and energy that is produced is the square of the speed of light according to Einstein's famous mass and energy equivalence equation. Research is necessary to find ways to induce fusion on microscopic scale and to control the energy produced without the destruction of the fusion apparatus. The reaction speed has to be under human control. The sun is burning bright through the fusion energy which is being produced in the extremely high temperature zone. Defence scientists of some developed countries have achieved controlled fusion in microscopic pellets for initiation of fission bombs. The fusion research has to be free from patenting control so that all countries may benefit and such research should be directly funded by the UN.

8.7 World Peace and Progress

There is a breeze blowing announcing the advent of spring in world affairs. World has reached the period when some further conscious effort for world peace might assure its permanence. The environment for progress can continue until humanity reaches its fulfilment in a guaranteed utopia based on cooperative effort of mankind and successes in science and technology. Immediate necessity is to remove irritants from consciousness of the ancient failures of races and nations and humanity can start from a clean slate with the knowledge that unless a natural calamity or renewed international hostilities erupt, world has millions of years for peace, progress and development. One of the common irritant happens to be superstitious beliefs and suspension of reason. Nehru advised India to embrace scientific approach. Democracy is the vehicle for national governments as well as international cooperation beginning with the growth of the UN. Decisions must be built up through discussions and acceptance of concerns of others for modification of the decision. Human happiness should be the criterion. India and many countries, we are sure, would be happy to provide secretariat for UN sponsored conferences especially concerning religion and philosophy and reforms to bring religions to incorporate latest results of science and technology so that people keep abreast of most reasonable theories and understand that all scientific conclusions are tentative and subject to verification and revision. Some guidelines are also necessary for economic and efficient use of media of mass communication. The necessity of this can strike anyone watching any common TV programme or rendering of news for public consumption. Men and women in future will have much more leisure for relaxation or building their body and developing their minds. Healthy lives and superior quality sports, and activity involving arts, music and crafts are there to choose from apart from quality professional work.

8.8 India's Civil and Military Doctrine

India's civil and military doctrine can be summed up in one word : "Peace". It is the peace believed in by a country ready to reach peaceful resolution of differences. The international anarchy already experienced by it has compelled it to attain nuclear deterrent. India displays periodically the hardware manufactured in India. India was one of the first few countries to attempt power generation from nuclear energy. The nuclear power accounts for about 50 per cent of requirements of certain energy starved regions of India. India supports IAEA in its task of controlling the functioning of the nuclear power generation. India will continue to make efforts towards complete disarmament and outlawing of weapons of mass destruction. Research on fast breeder reactors must continue for conserving nuclear materials. India has successfully experimented with thorium as nuclear fuel.

8.9 Radioactive Isotopes

Certain elements have a variety of nuclei differing in the number of neutrons. Such elements have more than one isotope. Some isotopes are radioactive and are called radio isotopes. There are some naturally occurring radioactive isotopes. Radioactive isotopes can also be created by the irradiation of some atoms. The radiation emitted by nuclear piles can be utilized for creating desirable isotopes. The radio isotopes are useful in agricultural research, in medical research and medical treatment, and as markers in metallurgical and high polymer researches. Since nuclear radiation can destroy certain bacteria and fungi without harming foodstuffs, such radiation often comes from exposed radio isotopes and is used for prolonging the shelf life of foodstuffs, *e.g.* vegetables, fruit or delay the ripening of some fruit. A battery of radio isotopes could be carried by long range fishing vessels in order to preserve freshness of the catch. Nuclear radiation is also useful in the treatment of cancer and other diseases. The Bhabha Atomic Research Centre at Mumbai carries on the business of bulky returnable lead containers to hospitals and other users. Seeds when irradiated last longer. Fruit and flowers can be irradiated before dispatch by air. The Indian Veterinary Research Institute has set up a factory to produce radiation treated vaccine for the lungworm disease. The radio-isotopes have wide applications in agricultural research or in industry and can be had from the Bhabha Atomic Research Centre, Mumbai.

8.10 Some Development Milestones

(a) Light Combat Aircraft. The project is nearing completion with the collaboration of American manufacturers. It has been a great exercise in Indian production of aircraft instruments and systems. India has also developed pilotless target aircraft which are now marketable.

(b) India is a leader in Remote Sensing and its applications in planning, agriculture, crop estimation, forest husbandry, weather forecasting, etc. India will be incorporating remote sensing and telemetry in their approaching moon shot in collaboration with other advanced countries like Russia, USA and Japan. This is likely to confirm the magnetic anomaly on the Rima Sirsalis ascribed by Nanda to a magnetic insert or rather an iron template exploded out of the earth around which the moon has been assembled in space close to the earth.

(c) The Uranium Corporation of India besides controlling procurement and storage of uranium and thorium is also active in advanced metallurgy like recovery of uranium. India in cooperation with France is working on use of thorium for nuclear energy. The existing plants still work on the uranium cycle.

(d) Defence Scientists of the Institute of Armament Technology have experimented with explosion welding and further work is being carried out at the IIT, Mumbai. Work on ion implantation for improving surface properties is going on in various laboratories.

8.11 Space Research and fall out

Space research started as an extension of rocketry and missile development. There was valuable fall out from space research, *e.g.* the development of the electronic hammer, ceramic bonded dry lubricants, fire proof coatings, advances in remote sensing, biometric telemetry, titanium technology, space age materials, *e.g.* strong flexible transparent materials, application of zirconium metal. India is now capable of designing and launching satellites for customers.

Since there is more activity now in space, agreed draft laws of working in space are now ready for adoption by the international community. An impotant clause is "stations, installations, equipment and space vehicles will be open to inspection by the representatives of any nation. The control of a hijacked plane or satellite has to be restored to the legitimate controller."

8.12 India's Economic Security

India's GDP in 2004-05 was Rs. 28.3 thousand crore. This made India the twelfth largest economy in the world with a GNP of $ 571 billion. In purchasing power terms, the adjusted GNP was $ 3062 billion. India is in a highly propitious phase. Currently, the economy is one of the fastest growing economies of the world. Agriculture absorbs about 60 per cent of the workforce. The increase percentage-wise in the agriculture sector is more than the expansion of manpower percentage. The employment in the service sector is high and increasing. Considerable relief has been given in this year's budget. There is continuing high cost for crude, and the country's Oil and Natural Gas Commission is expanding its exploration efforts inside India as well as in relatively unexplored regions of Africa and offshore in India. The leftists in the Parliament are vehemently opposed to any deal with the USA, but the government is confident to push the deal through in the national interest even without the support of the doctrinaire communists. The retail industry is one of the pillars of Indian economy and there is likely to be slow advance of corporate retail trade. The projection by Goldman Sachs of New York is that the Indian economy will overtake every country of Western Europe or Japan by 2025. India's growth is accelerating at present. India's coal reserves are the fourth largest in the world. Since liberalization, the government has approved significant banking reforms. The Right to Information Act passed into law is likely to bring down corruption significantly. The government is serious about redressing the complaints of consumers and customers of services including those run by the government. With more training, the efficiency of workers is rising. There is all-round progress being made by women; even Muslim women are confidently looking into the future. Genuine secularism and merit are going to be the watch-words of resurgent India.

9 Food Assurance and Sustainable Development

9.1 Introduction

A large proportion of the population is engaged in agriculture and rural professions. Priority consideration must remain remunerative work for all citizens. They are the labour of Marxist-Maoist terminology and can be prepared for the continuous revolution so very necessary in India according to Lok Nayak Jai Prakash Narain. The government gets to the ground level only through the actions of the bureaucracy or of the courts. The Chinese were the first to begin recruiting bureaucrats by examining all candidates for their grasp of the officially endorsed philosophy. We must also follow this principle, since any other way to secure a committed bureaucracy is not practical. The UPSC conducted selection examinations should have papers on Gandhian Thought, and sustainable development in agriculture and in power production. The judges have to be committed to the rule of law and the supremacy of the Constitution. Judges could also be recruited likewise and intermingling of careers of lawyers and judges can be dispensed with. Priority is to be accorded to infrastructure development and to education giving the status of an element in the infrastructure. The recently introduced development plans in the villages are popular and successful. Abundance of food and a commitment to development through education and constructive work are the keys to success. With continuous increase of population and increase in living standards along with limited cultivable land, intensive agriculture has to be the norm and it has to be sustained by the necessary agricultural planning and continuous soil enrichment. Experience of Israel has been a path breaker in management of water in the desert. For increasing industrial inputs into agriculture, the contribution of the various agricultural universities and their extension work has been extremely timely. For agriculture, regional knowledge centres are necessary since the soil and detailed climate of different regions is different. Every attention is being given to the sustainability of the agricultural inputs including a gigantic effort for rural electrification. USA began their modern period of development by setting up the Tennessee Valley Authority which has been the inspiration for Indian Bhakra-Nangal Project and many similar projects all over the world. Now the accent is on smaller power generation projects.

9.2 Food

Food is essential for life. It is only self-intoxicated sages who are rumoured to live on air and water only. Human body and mind are so structured that food intake can be reduced considerably (if chosen well) for healthy long life. With galloping population, it may become necessary to reduce food requirements for healthy men and women. The earth produces sufficiently to satisfy everyone's needs but there is not enough for greed. Too much and too rich food without required hard work or exercise is only an invitation to disease. Indian sages and savants prescribe simplicity in food. It is a myth that proteins from meat eating are necessary for human meals. Vegetarian diet is sufficient in all respects. Converting grains to animal feed and then eating the animal is less efficient than being a strict vegetarian. Majority of Indians are vegetarians without regarding fish eating as being non-vegetarian. Best food for babies is mother's milk and cow's milk is best supplement for babies or old people. World food supply is barely sufficient for world population. Affluent countries are eating much more than the world average. Any plans to economise on food resources have to start with affluent countries. First thing India accomplished after Independence was to become self-sufficient in food grains and then to be in a position to export them and help some other countries to alleviate their hunger. It was thanks to the efforts of Dr. M.S. Swaminathan and his colleagues in agriculture and hundreds of progressive farmers assisted by extensive agricultural extension work, that the green revolution happened in the case of wheat and later for rice. It is also a pleasure to record the outstanding initiation by Borlaugh in Mexico and the rice researches in Philippines. India is expecting a second green revolution soon with improved genetic varieties of seeds requiring lower quantities of irrigation and chemical inputs based now on organic fertilizers. The green revolution is being extended to rain dependent cultivated land. The Indian agriculture planning is well advanced and progressive. The same can be said about the active rural development projects and central projects for rural development like availability of bank loans on easy terms, trusting the peasants and subsistence agriculturists to engage in local cooperation to provide consolidated farms to practice mixed farming. Millions of small farms are to be treated as a resource for human welfare and productive and remunerative work without migration to the cities. The emphasis is on integrated farming using judicious development of tree plantations, rearing of cows, poultry and possibly bees and silk worms. Indian herbs and roots are the major providers of all pharmacopoeia. The Indian system of medicine propagates the use of whole herb plants and roots and believes their medicine preparations are better as they include many useful additions which are lost when chemically derived effective ingredients alone are extracted. They contend that the whole natural plant products are proven by experience on extensive cures in human beings when no adverse side effects occur that are often seen in the use of chemically formulated drugs using chemically purified plant products. There is international effort now proceeding to discover and prepare drugs from marine plants and animals. Food in abundance, industrial (including cottage and family industries) production, profitable trade and value added production are the engines of sustainable development.

Israel has shown the way to carry out intensive agricultural production in arid lands. New devices like spot irrigation reduce water requirements. The world is experiencing shortage in water supplies. In India too there is now a revival of community efforts to repair or dig new water tanks and avoid drainage of rainwater that could either better be in tanks for community use or be purposefully injected to augment groundwater. Every village and town now is on the way to develop *gobar* (animal or human excreta) gas and to erect water treatment plants. The nutrition experts (led by Prof. P.V. Sukhatma of Pune and the soul of first Community Kitchen started by a ladies cooperative) have certified that Indian customary vegetarian diet is nutritionally entirely satisfactory. The Ladies' Cooperative was preparing and reaching, more than 2,000 customers, hot nutritious vegetarian lunch everyday in their work places. This led the way to a new industry all over India of ladies initiative in providing hot lunches to office goers. Poultry is a good additional item for human consumption but poultry should be reared using farm waste as in Indian villages and not in giant factories leading to diversion of grains from direct human consumption. Fish meal provides additional item for poultry feed. Fish meal is prepared from discarded marine catch which is unfit for being thrown back into sea.

9.3 Fish and Poultry

It is beyond comprehension that religion should be confused with preference in food, clothing and language. Indians mostly prefer vegetarian food but everyone should choose without any compulsion to eat or not to eat meat. Vegetarian diet is rich enough in proteins and nutrients. Still it can be augmented by unfertilized poultry eggs without any spiritual disquiet. Most of the world population is meat eater. The dress code must be the wearer's choice so long as it is not offensive to others and is healthy and hygienic for the wearer. The scriptures of Bengal declare fish to be worthy of acceptance as food by vegetarians. It would be ostrich like to deny fish as food which is a universal table food. The fish catches, both marine as well as riverine or captive fish hatcheries are very important both for augmenting food resources and for export. The prawn cultivation in special sea water ponds and channels along the west coast of India is earning considerable amount of foreign exchange for India. Partaking of fish does not reduce any cultivated land for growing foodgrains for humans or animals. Marine fisheries along the Indian coasts are reaching their limits regarding sustainable annual catch; but India is not achieving or utilizing marine fish catches, that it ought to achieve looking at its length of the coastline and size of continental shelf. India has just started sea fishing. India has made remarkable progress in in-land fishing in rivers, tanks and lakes. There is considerable international as well as national research on getting desirable fish catches. Private efforts to spread fish production or to popularize fish diet in north Indian kitchens are commendable. There is valuable extension work for the fishing industry carried out by UK and the FAO and there are many popular periodicals on fishing both as an industry as well as sport. A large number of fisher folk are dependent on local marine fishing. Organizing fishing cooperatives will eliminate middlemen in the sale. Coconut, fish and coir are the life support of most islands and coastal populations around the north Indian ocean. The Department of Ocean Development in the Central Government at Delhi are acquiring oceanography and fisheries research vessels along with geotechnical ships for data acquisition for marine resources. Manganese nodules have been lifted from sea bottom by boomerang grabs by the National Institute of Oceanography a few hundred kilo metres south of the continental shelf in the centre of the north Indian Ocean. India has developed an easy acoustic method utilizing the fluctuation of the raw bottom echo (without automatic volume control) that could help in the selection of places and depths for rich net hauls. The food chain for small pelagic species like sardines, mackeral, anchovies and herring is a short one and these can occur in large shoals in the upwelling zones. Public sector has an increasing role in the exploitation of new fisheries. Organized fishing of oceanic tuna, mainly skipjack is being carried out around Lakshadweep islands and a large capacity canning plant has been set up on the Minicoy island. The FAO estimates that the surface fishery has the potential yield of 300,000 tonnes annually of skipjack. Compared to other oceans, Indian ocean fisheries are the least exploited. The near coast fisheries have reached a maximum sustainable level along the Malabar and Maharashtra coasts.

India has made remarkable progress in poultry farming in the last twenty years. Besides a few poultry raised by peasants without any extra expense than the permission to their few chicken to roam around the place picking up worms and stuff that has no other utility for the farmer, there have arisen now large commercial poultry farms all over the country. They have been advised to stay away from poultry food based on grains or oil cake that can be more fit for animal and human use. Poultry business in India now runs in crores of rupees. Poultry food factories mostly use fish meal or wastes from food factories.

9.4 Sustainable Development

Sustainable development is very important for countries which realize their limitations in land, numbers, skills, and commercial profits. For our size of population, we have limitations of every kind. Modern development in USA began with the setting up of the Tennessee Valley Authority. Now engineers are positive that giant dams are not the best solution for large scale development. These usually have silting problem and when the artificial reservoir silts up, the dam becomes useless and one has to think and build afresh smaller dams and bring large rivers under control in stages along its course. Egypt has already got this lesson regarding the river Nile. India will prefer embankments to ensure linking of rivers than obstructing the flow with large dams. The

Indian system, of guiding rainwater to flow into tanks built and maintained by large villages and urban habitations, should be multiplied. The old canals and tanks got silted up and went into disrepair unnoticed on account of long periods of anarchy and alien rule. Now even the capital Delhi is nostalgic about the Mughal canals and tanks around the site of Delhi. If we had kept those tanks and canals in good condition, that would have provided a good example of sustainable development. The subsistence agriculture in small plots could not produce enough for our galloping population. The rural population in their spare time engaged themselves in cottage industries of all kinds including small foundries for iron and other metal ware. They could thus augment their income. After impoverishment through trade getting inverted to imports of all kinds, the remedy that appeared first in Bengal and later through the Gandhian organizations for cottage industries all over India was the slogan of *charkha* (spinning wheel) and *swadeshi* (made in own land) products. In spite of human memory being short, India will do well to remember this and not lose once again its moorings because of flooding of goods into India by the globalization process and killing the local production of many goods which may be of lower quality in the international market. The effort has to be made that our goods also are of international standard and can be had on comparative terms. Certain sacrifices may be necessary to keep our small scale industries afloat and should be gladly embraced. We should learn from the Chinese and the Japanese how to improve the quality of our products. Bold initiatives and creativity are required besides salesmanship. The disunity in India in the 17th and the 18th centuries was our undoing. The India-Pakistan distrust will not be to the advantage of either country in this subcontinent. The answer really lies in the strong bonds being created among all the citizens of India whatever be their religion or language. When one of the authors was a student in USA, he had a close friend, a Muslim living in the next room. After more than one year of friendship and mutual help in sickness or companionship in campus activities, the Muslim friend exclaimed that he was certain that his Hindu friend would make a good Muslim and was surprised why this had not happened. It took a few days to talk to him about the catholicity of outlook of the Hindus and relative freedom from leading a stereotyped life. His final comment was that he has lived his entire life in the Punjab but had never learnt about the real features of Hinduism. To achieve better integration among the Hindus and Muslims of India, what is needed is easy lessons in school textbooks about the values for becoming better human beings in each religion. The reader should excuse the above digression since Hindu-Muslim unity in India is part of sustainable development in our villages. In our village communities, the producers and consumers are closely associated and depend on happy unstressed living. The Indian state is fully aware of advantage of decentralization of the development process and decentralizing the availability of capital for small scale industries, cooperative farming and the organization of small scale industries. The concept of some sufferer pointing out corruption to be mended by some official, is giving way to the superior authority itself discovering through its agents and free press, the corrupt links in administration and mending them. This is a good place also to describe the Hindu concept of nature worship. An ancient tree is decorated with garlands and is believed to fulfil devotee's wishes. Cow is regarded as foster mother as it is the source of milk, the preferred food for children next to mother's milk. Small seedlings grown at home of foodgrains are worshipped on the festival of Dussehra in autumn. The Hindus love their mountains and rivers and show it by the worship of deities representing them, but have only now reminded themselves that the holy rivers have to be kept clean. From Ashoka's days they have been taught to be vegetarian. Only now scientists and dieticians are agreeing with this view. We are repentant that we could not persevere in the preservation of adequate forest cover. The recommended cover is 25 per cent, but in India it is only 15 per cent. Energetic efforts are being made to stop any cutting of trees and many buildings and roads are redesigned to avoid felling of trees. It is amazing that the Hindu Law books mention severe punishment for any reckless cutting of trees. The sacred groves of South Asia provide buffer areas with wild growth. Man is to be nourished by nature, but he in return has to nourish nature. There is overfishing in near shore fisheries and sea food supply is continuously dwindling requiring periodical rest to various fisheries. Rice supply is difficult to augment but additional quantity of other grains, pulses and fish and poultry products may be available. As preparation of this change, the food and dietary habits of rice eaters have to be modified now than later.

It is a wonder that traditional subsistence agriculture has been keeping up the productivity of Indian soil for thousands of years. The secret lies in the use of organic manure from cow-dung, plant and food wastes. There is going to be additional task for agriculture to grow diesel generating plants. Any intensive agriculture can best be carried out by improving our collection of organic wastes for making good manure and where necessary to assure supply of mineral nitrates and phosphates for which raw material is in abundant supply. Intensive efforts are needed following Sanjay Gandhi's slogan of planting trees. The need of this is staring one in the face when one sees the hills of Maharashtra denuded of all trees from base to top. One wishes to bring wild fruit trees to the region which is quite possible if there are heroes in Maharashtra like Mr. Appleseeds of the USA. There is ample room for more activism like Bhaktipheri or devotional tours of villages by knowledgeable town folk. In mixed farming, the animal dung and poultry droppings become preferred manure for cereal and vegetable production. Grassroots democracy means decentralization of farming decisions to the district level. Sustained development requires not only decentralization but decentralization of power plants and extensive use of solar energy. The hunger for power consumption is increasing by leaps and bounds as it must when every village is to be connected by road or rail. Nuclear energy for peaceful purposes is a solution but the equipment and some critical parts are manufactured as monopoly of advanced countries. The developing countries should now gear up for cooperative manufacture of such critical parts and machines.

9.5 Impact of New Technologies

Every nation has to keep abreast of new technologies so that full advantage can be taken for economy in pursuit of development objectives and also to guard against adverse effects if any. Considerable scientific manpower is now engaged in biotechnology. Apart from academic pursuits, genetic engineering is now sought for gene modification in seeds to obtain disease resistant varieties or for early or late maturity, and more yield of grains or fruit. Genetic engineering might also lead to substitutes for sugar, vanilla, cocoa etc., which can affect Indian export of sugar and vanilla or cocoa from agriculture. One famous physical chemist had reduced his food to a few tablets prepared in his chemistry laboratory but he died before he could attract a following. There was recently a spurt in filing patents for seed producing plants endowed with special qualities but which had also been observed in nature through long evolutionary changes. India is strongly suspicious of such grant of intellectual property rights for formal inventions when the same knowledge is traditionally existing. Biological processes for the production of plants and animals with new traits are to be studied for the common good and such results should be excluded from patentability.

There are so many inventions and machines that save labour. Simple devices for the deletion of hard physical fatigue in many agricultural tasks are most welcome and even bullock cart associated agriculture is taking to such simple machines if their virtue is demonstrated to the simple peasant. Agriculture can benefit also by high science and technology. The costs and infrastructure of technical training can be borne only by "industrial" scale agriculture. Computers prescribe the nature, timing and quantity of manure and quantity and number of irrigation water inputs. Even spray nozzle for watering the lawn is a technological labour saving device.

When computers start running such machines and inputs, we approach the invention of agricultural robots. The peasant was reduced to a cheap robot in the feudal and capitalist society. In the future computer age of agriculture, the peasant will rule a number of technological robotic slaves. When we reach this stage, most of the agricultural labour will have continuous free time to indulge in cultural pursuits and there would be an efflorescence of art and literature, philosophy and technology never dreamt of so far. In preparation for such a future, scientific education must begin for the entire population. India is silently engaged on this project. Social peace and pastimes also have science and technology applications. Radio isotopes could be used for preservation of fruit and fish thus assuring more trade in perishable items.

Apart from new gene manipulation technologies, biodiversity alone is an asset. Under the tree borne oilseeds integrated development scheme, initial plantations for reaching commercial scale of Jetropha Curcas and Karanja for bio-diesel extraction have been planted in many places. The agricultural sector in India, and Africa may especially benefit. Dr. Swaminathan has warned that before investing in bio-diesel plantations commercially, economical return of diesel must be assured to avoid disappointment later. Commercial horticulture has been started in many states and has a great potential because of the growing internal as well as an external market supported by low rates for airfreightage for cut flowers. Some states are particularly assisting in the cultivation and marketing of medicinal and aromatic plants and oilseed bearing trees. There is scope for more enterprise in these particularly in Himachal, Uttrakhand, Sikkim and the North East India and the continuation of the success in West Bengal and Karnataka.

Nanotechnology or the technology utilizing the special properties of materials when these are composed of nano (10^{-9} m) sized particles is attracting considerable funds in developed countries. It has many industrial and military applications. The new technology is expected to spawn new export oriented industries. Nanotechnology originated in instrumentation connected with the activation of thermonuclear bombs and soon numerous applications for surface treatments and surface strength of materials and bearings followed. It has applications in development of various sensors and high energy propellants and coatings of airframes for low radar reflectivity. India has kept abreast of modern developments in this versatile field.

Sustainable developments are very much dependent on the adoption of new tehnologies, new instruments and harnessing of new knowledge to develop new skills and new applications.

10 Development of Modern Industries

10.1 Introduction

India as mentioned earlier is surrounded by natural barriers and could easily be isolationist and happy with its stage of development in cottage industries and new found development of metal and glass working two thousand years ago. All material resources for simple living were available. India was not jealous of any other country. It had trade and travel relations with the rest of the world, but this was not to be. Many not so fortunate people sought migration into India. The migrants if they sought better life and came in peace were always welcome like the later day immigrants from Iran known today as Indian Parsis, Tajiks, Tibetans, Nepalis, and Sufis from West Asia, or the Ethiopeans as recruits in the armies of certain kings in India. Some came in aggressively, but India absorbed them and they became defenders of Indian territories from later intruders. Thus the Indian territory became home to a mixture of tribes and languages with a common culture of belief in human brotherhood, love of nature and love for the land of their adoption. They had a belief in life after death and rewards and retribution for all good or evil deeds. Thus India became culturally a nation. It developed Sanskrit language for the learned and Prakrit for the general public. India practiced widespread agriculture and cottage industries for trade. Its wealth attracted greedy interest of the tribes outside. The greed was glorified as religious zeal to spread the worship of one God not tolerating worship through idols. This zeal was translated into attacks for looting the wealth of India and to break the idols in every nook and corner of this country. India withstood these attacks for five hundred years without realizing the gravity of the situation that being friendly to all they had allowed themselves little preparedness for defence or accumulation of latest arms and fire power except for a brief interlude when they expelled Greek intruders in their midst. Similar situation prevailed in China who at least built their Great Wall at a certain stage. When India after a long struggle was ready to throw off the earlier Asian aggression, a new threat arose from distant imperialists from Europe who had come to India as traders but who joined in the struggles of many kingdoms in India. The British won this struggle through their belief in their superior culture and superior leadership. In the 18th century the British and other European traders had come to buy things in India with European gold and silver and then sell these at profit in Europe. Besides sugar and spices they bought yarn and cloth, precious stones and ornaments, hand tools, metalware including Indian steel and other artifacts from Indian handicrafts. India was the workshop of the world for a long time. The establishment of the British Empire in India opened the doors for profits and illegal loot of India's wealth. This wealth was the nourishment of new learning, inventions and advances in science and technology in Great Britain. Science and entrepreneurship is a hot house growth. These require peace, adventurous spirit and social and financial support. England could provide these and in addition provide captive markets. Where there was no market, they created one by aggression and gun boat diplomacy as in China for their opium manufactured by cheap labour in India. India which was exporting many articles of everyday use, started importing needles to road rollers from Great Britain. India which used to manufacture their own bows and arrows, spears and swords, rockets and large guns (a 19th century large gun stands on display at the centre of Lahore now in Pakistan), now started even importing the oil for cleaning their rifles. India used to build sailing ships for the British, became dependent on imports and was lagging in engineering for communications and even for defence.

Many able administrators and dedicated missionaries that came to India in the wake of British victory acted as a valuable change agents and awakened the dormant scientific spirit of Indians, particularly of the Hindus of Bengal or the Parsis of Gujarat. The leaders of India resolved to build unity, scientific knowledge, to abolish superstition and follies masquerading as religion. Indian renaissance started in Kolkata. Many modern industries were started there. Some great innovators and leaders of industry arose before independence, sometimes benefiting from the Gandhian slogan of "*Swadeshi*", *i.e.* the label of 'made in India' and sometimes riding on the pressing need for defence stores urgently required for the British empire's preparation for fighting the two world wars. Names of Parsi entrepreneurs are Tata and Godrej, who are world famous. The Indian Association for the Cultivation of Science was established in 1870. Dwarkanath Tagore established an indigo factory and also pioneered in spinning and ship building industries. Kolkata had many textile and pharmaceutical factories. Kanpur, Ahmedabad and Chennai became centres of many modern industries before independence in 1947.

10.2 Industrial Development since 1947

Since India got independence from the British Empire without any armed revolt, for quite some time India believed that no foreign nation would bother to attack India who could prevail over the strongest imperialist country of the day. The army was in fact neglected both regarding service conditions or regarding its arms and equipment. The attention was more focused on food self-sufficiency and improving the earnings of rural families by expansion of cottage industries. Still under the revolutionary stir in favour of Indian made cloth and other articles of use, industrial manufacture of household articles expanded. Many British manufacturers started subsidiaries in India or expanded their collaborators' enterprises. Particular expansion was of chemical and electrical manufactures. Soon India was making and using Indian made aeroplanes, trucks, cars and scooters and Indian made diesel engines for pulling railway trains. Many portions of railway tracks were electrified and Indian made electrical railway engines were also in use. India needed more steel and more electricity. All the developed countries did not wish to share their advances in steel making with India. They also criticized the choice by India for developing heavy industries since small scale industries held a promise of more jobs. Due to constraints of the international situation and apparent ganging up of China and Pakistan, and with USA leaning towards Pakistan as a relatively smaller "innocent" country, India found the Soviet Union most considerate. The Soviet Union permitted their latest steel technology to be made available to India at reasonable terms. Soon a treaty of friendship was signed between the two countries that was very beneficial to India. After the breaking up of the Soviet Union, Russia is again following the Soviet policy of frendship with India which also continues to cherish the Soviet friendship for India. (It was under great strain when the Soviet Union attacked Afghanistan — a very good friend of India). A spurt in industrialization followed with the Russian technology and design in the lead. Seeing Indian industrialization forging ahead, Canada, Germany, UK and France also began transferring technology and development funds to India. India also began exporting industrial goods. The goods from small scale electronic industries exported to the Soviet Union included floppy disc drives, semi-conductors, computer peripherals, electronic motors, capacitors, computer software, magnetic recording heads, mica plates, telecommunication cables, carbon film resistors, etc. India had developed textile and fibre industries and a well stocked profession of chemical engineers. India soon got to its proper place in this age of tailored materials. High performance materials were designed using metal, carbon, textile, or ceramic fibres using metallic or plastic matrix. The chemical industry has produced innumerable plastic materials. The structure variables are the chemical nature of the monomer and the physical nature of the polymer comprising chain length, side chains, grafts, metal bridges, cross linking pattern, and the nature of fillers, and subsequent heat treatment, the stacking pattern, crystallinity processing parameters and bulk shape. Many industries were set up by private capital for the requirements of road building, expansion of railways, agro chemicals, household goods, etc.

Continuous scientific and engineering support is required for rapid growh of industries. Far sighted Nehru established new R&D establishments with support of able administrators around the year of independence. Defence R&D Organization among others was the nursery of many industries. Aerospace, electronics and semi-conductor industries have been the beneficiary through availability of a pool of trained staff. Recent contributions include the subjects of digital IC technology or the start of carbon nano tube based device development. Carbon fibres were first developed in India in Defence Materials Research Laboratory at Kanpur and their know-how was taken up by the National Physical Laboratory at Delhi when the development further was assigned to them by the inter-ministerial coordinators. From Defence Production efforts, the culture of laboratory scale and pilot plant scale production spread to other laboratories and private industry. Industrial advance is visible by nuclear submarine with its armaments fully developed and built in India and inducted in the Indian Navy in 2009.

10.3 Industrial Infrastructure

Even as early as 1935, much before India's independence Nehru had set up a planning commission responsible to the Congress, his political party. A chain of national laboratories, with competence to develop any original idea to a pilot plant stage, was established. A second great Indian to be remembered in this context is Prof. Homi Bhabha who set up the Atomic Energy Commission (AEC) and was the first head of the Tata Institute of Fundamental Research at Mumbai. He was responsible for advancing nuclear research leading to electric power generation. Later on India could develop the competence mainly on their own to develop atom bombs, and production and use of nuclear isotopes. The AEC assisted the government to plan and set up Bharat Electronics Ltd. at Bangalore that has developed many firsts in applications and manufacture of semi-conductors and has advanced the electronic industries supported by the Department of Electronics of the government. India soon became self-sufficient in the manufacture of radars, computers, avionics and instrumented satellites.

Another name to be remembered is that of V.K. Krishna Menon, the Defence Minister of India. He and Prof. D.S. Kothari, the first scientific adviser to the Defence Minister, established a string of laboratories dedicated to defence research and production in India of defence equipment and arms. A second push to defence production came when missiles began to be designed and produced under the primary leadership of APJ Abdul Kalam who later became the President of India. The other important contributors to defence production were the Hindustan Aeronautics for the production of many types of civil and military aircrafts, and the expanded dockyards at Kolkata, Visakhapatnam and Mumbai which are designing and producing men-of-war of various sizes and equipped with suitable armaments including rockets, radars and sonars. Naval research laboratories at Mumbai, Cochin, and Visakhapatnam are fully integrated in the naval defence preparedness programmes. An India made submarine as well as a rebuilt aircraft carrier have been possible besides mine sweepers, destroyers and missile boats. The Indian ordnance factories have been functioning for over a century making all kinds of ammunition, tanks and anti-tank missiles, guns for the three services etc. Defence production organization has many test and trial ranges for evaluation of new arms before introduction into service use.

10.4 Government Industrial Policy

The Indian industrialization has been achieved by pragmatic continuous efforts to industrialize in the national interest for generating remunerative work for the vast under- or un-employed individuals and households in India. The problem still exists and demands ever more attention. A second imperative was realization of security and survival in the anarchic world of self-centred nations still enmeshed in power politics which has no principles except a myopic view of self-interest. Many countries after Second World War were split at the convenience of the victors, *e.g.* Germany, Korea, Palestine, South Africa, Indonesia, Congo. India was also partitioned creating Pakistan perhaps for a future use against India which might turn out to be an inconvenient country for the imperialists. India-Pakistan differences have continued to multiply even when Pakistan got the best terms after losing to India in two major wars begun by it. In a similar situation any other victor would have ensured that Pakistan should not constitute a threat in future, but India had an inherent hope that Pakistan would soon give up the company of the imperialist powers and take to natural response to India's friendly stance. India also realized that the conditions that created Pakistan were still running strong. There was also the priority of reaching food grain self-sufficiency. For creating Indian defence industry of significance, the first priority was to expand steel and power production. The assistance for this, first came from the Soviet Union (and later also from Canada, Germany, UK and the USA). Heavy Electricals Ltd. was set up at Bhopal for making heavy electrical machinery and the Bhilai Steel Plant grew up with Soviet assistance.

Private capital in India was not strong enough to start capital intensive heavy industries or to build atomic energy resources and bureaucracy could not be trusted to spread itself thin over myriads of factories required to meet growing needs of the Indian population. The government therefore sought to run a mixed economy permitting both public sector and private sector. Both have prospered. With current globalization activity and liberalization of administrative policies in India regarding industrialization and the inflow of foreign capital and easy repatriation of profits overseas, setting up and operation of manufacture of industrial goods has advanced by leaps and bounds.

10.5 An Overview of Current Industrial Production

One may mention large scale factories such as thermal, hydrothermal and gas based electric power production of 10,000 Megawatts installed capacity; installed capacity for manufacture of automobiles, tractors, 2/3 wheelers is a million units per annum; and for steel production 38 million tonnes per annum. India operates 60 per cent of global mica trade. Geological Survey of India and the Indian Bureau of Mines assist mining enterprises for coal, lignite, bauxite, chromite, copper, lead and zinc, kaolin, limestone, marble etc. Chemical industry has a great spread over types of products as well as geographical spread. Some major concerns are fertilizer industries (National Fertilizers Ltd. has five factories in the Punjab, Rashtriya Chemicals and Fertilizers have five factories in Maharashtra and Gujarat, FACT produces nitrogen, or phosphate in Kerala, Madras Fertilizers in Chennai etc.). Institute of Pesticide Formulation and Technology has been established at Gurgaon, and Indian Dyes and Pesticides in West Bengal. Many industries have state collaboration like Indian Drugs and Pharmaceuticals, and some are wholly Public Sector like Hindustan Antibiotics Ltd. at Pimpri. The Bengal Chemical and Pharmaceuticals was set up in 1981. To assist plastic industries there is the Central Institute of Plastic Engineering and Technology with twelve extension centres. There are a number of factories manufacturing polymers or plastomers and elastomers, raw materials as well as cast or extruded etc. products. India has been specially successful in increasing production and export of light engineering goods. There are 128 large cement plants with production reaching 152 million tonnes per annum. 10 per cent of world supply of leather and leather goods is from India. India is almost self-sufficient for its paper needs. About one million tonnes of soaps and detergents are produced per annum. About a million families are engaged in sericulture and producing all the five varieties of silk.

Certain areas have been reserved for the Public Sector like

Atomic energy and Railway rolling stock. Licence from government is still required for the following subjects: distillation and brewing, tobacco, electronics, aerospace, defence explosives, defence equipment, industrial explosives, matches, hazardous chemicals, certain listed drugs and chemicals. The automatic route exists for setting up industries under FDI (Foreign Direct Investment) excluding certain areas, *e.g.* tea industry, operation of satellites, print media, oil refineries, airports, broadcasting, banking, insurance, mining of diamonds and precious stones etc. (The accent is on advancement of industrialization but preservation of long range freedom of action in the national interest.) Privilege of FDI is denied for following subjects: retail trading, atomic energy, lottery, gambling and betting, real estate, plantations other than tea. Among other important public sector undertakings, one can mention Mineral Exploration Corporation with headquarters at Nagpur which was set up in 1967 with constituents like the National Aluminum Company, Bharat Gold Mines and Hindustan Copper.

10.6 Relative Armed Strength of China, India and Pakistan

Security is the prime concern of any nation. India had suffered needless attacks from two neighbours China and Pakistan. These attacks accomplished nothing for the aggressors. India had always regarded China as a cultured friend and continues to deepen its friendship, but China has been dragging its feet in finalizing an agreed boundary demarcation with India when the principles determining the boundary have been already sorted out. From the start India was disposed towards Pakistan as a natural ally, sharing a natural common habitat with centuries of togetherness in the past but for religious or rather anti-religious poison injected into Hindus and Muslims of India in 1919 by the imperialists by imposing colonial democracy with comunal electorates. India with full responsibility agreed to the creation of Pakistan so that the remaining country carries forward the torch of India to enlighten all to live in peace and cooperation. India also learnt a lesson that reasonable armed strength is essential to meet any aggression till the friendly countries can possibly extend help directly or through the UN. For this in view, we are giving the relative armed strength of the three nations under discussion from open literature :

Item	*Pakistan*	*India*	*China*
Defence Expenditure	$ 3.3 billion	13.6 billion (3.4%of GDP)	40 billion (5.4 % of GDP)
Armed Forces Manpower	600,000	1,150,000	2,200,000
Tanks	2,300	3,500	9000
Towed Artillery	1,600	4,200	14,500
Combat Aircraft	430	774	3,500
Attack Helicopters	20	32	NA
Aircraft Carrier	0	1	0
Submarines (Diesel Powered)	10	19	62
Submarines Nuclear powered with missiles	0	1	6 (Strategic Missile Force)
Destroyers	7	16	18
Frigates	8	18	36
Missile Craft	8	6	88 plus air launched cruise missiles
Armed Forces			

Security assurance can come only by extending a hand of friendship and removing the reasons for ill will between nations. In the absence of any external security cover, any disproportional increase of arms acquisition by any player portends aggression for the weaker neighbour. The world has witnessed the invention and then proliferation of atomic bombs. The possession of atomic weapons, particularly the ability of preserving some weapons for a second strike after absorbing the first initial atomic bomb attack from the enemy, is a correct deterrent. Pakistan and India became nuclear powers primarily to have their own deterrent when they were not treaty bound to a big power to give them such protection. In fact treaties are no longer held sacred and have been flouted easily. Both India and Pakistan possess some atomic bombs which can deter them from attacking each other. The other nuclear powers in the region are USA and China. India's nuclear arsenal is not a deterrent to either of these countries. India's policy declaration of not being the first to use such weapons is disarming enough from India's foreign policy of friendship and co-existence since its existence. USA did drop atom bombs on Japan knowing full well that the Japanese and the axis powers were not so armed, but USA. and the axis powers were already at war. Germany and Japan, if the war continued, might also have succeeded in making a similar bomb and with their record of raising the intensity of war on earlier occasions, any delay would certainly have resulted in exchange of atomic bomb thrusts devastating all countries. For further assurance, until the UN can be strong enough with a mandate from the whole world and full disarmament or placing of all bombs and the production facilities for weapons grade uranium, at the disposal of the UN, India will be engaged in achieving the second strike capability including the necessary production and deployment of nuclear powered, missile loaded and practically invincible submarines. It is best now to start serious world negotiations to have the international community jointly control nuclear arms production and all stockpiles in order to liberate the nations, big and small, from the fear of an anarchic world. USA has mooted the plan to permit cooperation with India by the advanced countries in the peaceful uses of atomic energy. World advancement needs full spirited pursuit by all nations and an assurance of continued peace.

Many of the advanced naval ships are only begun to be made in India. The same can be said about aeroplanes and satellites. The first world countries are well ahead, but whatever India learns to make, the knowledge will be readily shared with the developing world within the terms of international agreements regarding passing on such technologies to others. India has made many weather forecasting and communication satellites. It has the giant rockets for launching satellites and hopes to be in the forefront of commercial fallout from satellite and space probe experience. Same holds for Indian initiative in power production from atomic piles. It is even now in a position to export experimental atomic reactors.

Some of the sophisticated weapon systems and acquisition electronics have been indigenized. India is abreast of new technologies: electronics, genetic manipulation, scientific exploration etc. India is all attentive to the prediction by an Indian scientist of the site on the moon ready for mining of ready made steel and many valuable elements. India has discovered certain areas on the sea bottom in the Indian ocean which has abundance of manganese nodules ready to be lifted and processed requiring abundance of electrical power for off-shore work.

11 Higher Education, Arts and Post Modern Exports

11.1 Introduction

In the glorious ancient and medieval periods of Indian history learning was of Sanskrit or Persian texts and learning by rote of religious texts in Sanskrit or Arabic. Medicine, philosophy and astronomy were taught by learned masters to one or a few favoured disciples. Printing had not yet begun. Books were rare handwritten copies owned by the teachers. The princes of territories large or small supported learning as well as the Brahmans and monks handsomely. When the native rulers lost to invaders, first to the Iranians-Arabs and then to the Turkish-Afghan tribes, the state support to Brahmans languished, and higher learning was only a pursuit of a few learned individuals. Routine agriculture, handicrafts continued and as stated elsewhere, India stayed a rich country with practical skills in agriculture, pottery, metal mining and casting, spinning and weaving, trade and marine activity etc. Architecture continued to give masterpieces. Sculpture and murals were commissioned by temples. Palaces and tombs also had calligraphy and marble inlay embellishments. When we think of any resurgence in learning, it has to be understood in a new environment of activity of Christian missions and European civil servants who ruled from the 18th century followed by Indian civil servants and politicians glorifying in the changes brought about by the British change agents. Resurgence in education, science and technology is now the flowering of the transplanted European higher education particularly in science and technology as well as the analytical skills in European learning. Many Indian universities followed closely the ways of the British and later the American universities. University education is secular and democratic. With independence, new strength has also reached Brahmanical learning and learning based on Islamic Madrasa culture but this hardly matters for the resurgence bringing about industrialization.

11.2 Science and Technology

New discoveries in agricultural sector or in the application of high science and technology to our handicrafts and the technical advancement necessary for expanded trade and extended means of transport and communication, are the consequence of increasing spread of science and technology education and training. Most higher learning is supported by state fully or by giving annual or periodic grants and some funds for approved projects of study and research. Many of the universities and institutions of advanced studies are of the world class like similar institutions in the United Kingdom or in the USA. Many bright students from the second world come to the Indian universities for higher education and Indian teachers and professors are readily recruited by affluent countries. Students from the first world find it more economical to get the first medical degree in India and then pass some professional examinations in a couple of years to become qualified to occupy medical jobs or to engage in medical practice there. Many dedicated foreigners come repeatedly to India to learn Indian and foreign languages, Indian system of Ayurvedic medicine and Yoga discipline for non-formal health related practice in their own country or for self-medication. With independence, new vigour has also come to Brahamanical learning and Muslim Madrasas and Sufi philosophy, but this hardly concerns our subject of industrial production, post-modern exports or the resurgence of arts. The *Madrassa* type training could be harnessed for creating repugnance to corruption and attachment to democracy and humanism.

In developing countries education could be regarded as an element of infrastructure for advancement along with air, road and rail communications, so that there is development of education along with communications. Some enthusiasts like to measure progress in science and technology from the share of annual tally of Nobel prizes coming to products of Indian universities and Indian institutions. So far such share is poor, but the reason is social pressure for applied research particularly which enhances agricultural and industrial production. Advance in basic sciences is very much a hot house effort and the device of substantial scholarships and evidence of trust in the potential of bright individuals is essential. The eminent scientists engaged in post-graduate teaching and research have to be assured of life-long engagement and given control of some long term fellowships for their chosen disciples. The society must find ways to give respect and recognition to scholars as was evidently done in ancient times where the rulers felt honoured by the visit of a scholar or a philosopher. At present respect exists only for riches. Another deficiency is in the calibre of editors of learned journals who cannot choose wisely their referees and only want a "pass or fail" verdict from them. The referees and editors have to support budding and creative contributions by guiding these to the full reach of their potential. Unfortunately India still lacks independent and far seeing editors of scientific journals. Only obviously valid papers are published usually toeing creative work from outside. Some evidence of recognition is there for work supported by eminent scientists in the BARC, or the prestigious research establishments. Late starters like Russia, Japan, China and European continental countries also face these difficulties. Bureaucratic ascendancy too neglects creativity as long as they can.

Indian higher education has now its alumni carrying on their work with credit in every field. Every international symposium or conference has Indian contribution of high standard. Last year for example, the utility of the blue green algae as a potential bio-fertilizer was established in rice cultivation in a sustainable manner. An

Indian scientist has advanced the chemical clearing of oil spills on the ocean, so harmful to marine life and the use of beaches for recreation. In a Bangalore hospital, a successful transplant of an engineered bladder has been carried out on a child. Contributions of a high order have been made to solid state chemistry and to theoretical properties of molecular clusters. Intensive study of elementary particle encounters in ionization chambers is going on in many universities. An Indian scientist has revolutionized the understanding of the earth's interior as well as the origin of planetary satellites. Space research and remote sensing are attracting many scientists, engineers and planners. Meteorological research, including meteorological instrumentation and production of charts is a crowded scientific vocation in India. Indian software scientists are very productive. Computer recognition of working instructions given verbally is now possible even in Indian languages. This will give an impetus to development of household robots for use in India or for export. Scientists of a defence laboratory published the last paper on corrosion prediction from knowledge of meteorological factors for any particular area putting a lid on a plethora of similar attempts by other corrosion scientists. Similarly a final paper was published by an Indian scientist on the confusing subject of fluctuation of intensity of sound signals in the oceans. He also gave an interesting paper on the subject of possibility of an economical fish catch in any given area of the ocean. The method needed only the analysis of sea bottom echoes and took about a couple of minutes. It is unfortunate that there was no follow up of marketing a simple electronic instrument that would have been welcomed in fishing exploratory efforts all over the world. Indian scientists have published pioneering work on sea roughness.

New fellowships are now coming up in India for financing promising scholars to work at institutions of their choice. Real trusting fellowships as in UK are still not available in which a person once selected can keep on working in the field of his choice for as long as he/she wishes. The support annually renewed smells of vacillation and doubt on the part of the institution. The booming economy is perhaps a consequence of success of implementation of current economic theory and its mastery. Higher incomes and recognition are encouraging people to have pride in their work and so perform with higher efficiency. Customers are no longer regarded as a nuisance and even government departments are responding to complaint redressal with promptness. Legally enforced transparency and zealous guarding of democracy is leading to greater efficiency and conscientious discharge of duties.

The scientists need to know about related work of other scientists as soon as possible. In USA certain private parties distribute free reprints of important papers as these are published to certain scientists and institutions of their choice. This service could easily be undertaken by the Indian documentation centres set up by the government with expert assistance of learned societies and academies.

Considerable work is being done in bio-technology which is the current new technology for intensive theorctical and practical interest. Plant cells will be used for the accelerated production of natural products. Biocatalysis will require isolated enzymes. Biocatalysis can produce desired spatial patterns in polymers.

Stem cell research would lead to cure and understanding of complex diseases. "Stem cells are immature clonogenic self renewing proginator cells that have the capacity to give rise to mature functioning cells." Such cells can be derived from bone marrow or the umbilical cord. First stem cell transplantation centre has been set up at Chennai for treatment of Leukemia. The Bangalore based Cryostem Inc has stem cell project for the Malayasia Stem Life Corp.

Nano-technology, utilizing the special properties of materials composed of nano sized particles is attracting a lot of research effort. It has practical applications in the development of various sensors, in high energy propellants, or coatings for airframes for low radar reflectivity.

Radioactive isotopes can be created by irradiation from nuclear piles of targets of selected elements. The radio-isotopes are useful in agricultural research, in medicine and engineering. India is in the market for selling rechargeable radio isotopes for furthering academic and industrial research. DNA fragments are under investigation as biological computer component. Semi-conductor complex at Chandigarh is experimenting with MEMS (Micro Electro-Mechanical Devices).

The main concern of the technical manpower is support to industrial production and development of new stores and instruments. Electronics and electrical engineers have upgraded avionics of many existing aircraft, installed new air-borne electronic navigational and detection devices; they have installed computers for digital map generation and voice recognition systems. Anti-submarine warfare system made in India costs one-tenth of the cost of the imported one. Fuel cell assisted battery operated vehicle has been developed. The first true hovercraft was built in India in 1972. A bomb disposal robot has been developed and will be a normal equipment in fire fighting stations. In the development of robotics, Indian engineers have developed a remote operated vehicle as well as a robotic arm with six degrees of freedom. Programmes exist for the study of terrain relief and mapping of moisture content of ground.

Indian Institute of Nuclear Medicine has made important contributions to radiation therapy in the treatment of cancer. Hard magnets have been developed by spark plasma sintering of tin-cobalt-iron powders. Nano-technology developed in certain defence laboratories abroad has been learnt for numerous future uses in production of microchips and integrated circuits.

Certain similarity of practice of scientific research and practice of meditation and spiritual quest is apparent. Both are the preserve of dedicated individuals. Physics is not yet settled in its fundamentals and neither is spirituality. Scientific problems require enormous expenditure of human effort as well as large scale investments in equipment and high energy machines which enjoins multi-national collaboration especially in the subjects of astronomy and astrophysics, oceanography and space science. These are the subjects where the fallout of basic researches also benefits defence preparedness in the modern world of purblind nations. The top science problems according to Prof. Ginzburg of Russia are the study of large molecules, thermo-nuclear fusion, quantum crystals, plasma collapse and particle interactions at high energies. A study of gravitational waves will give a boost in the parallel problem of the emergence of a new thought in the swarm of neurons in the brain.

11.3 Resurgence of Arts

India has an open door policy for students and scientists of all nations to collaborate with Indian scientists and institutions. Talented artists are spreading their knowledge to other countries by blending Indian music and dance with foreign idiom.

Philosophers have defined architecture as frozen art. Ancient Indian art frozen in the cave temples or temple pagodas of south India or the standardized architecture of north Indian temples and many monuments in marble spell architectural resurgence. After independence, a load of puritanical convention imposed by foreign hypocrisy was removed and India surged forward to make up for lost time. Now every hamlet takes pride in having a temple, a mosque or a gurdwara with at least one tall minaret, or a dome. The recently built Akshardham temple and the Bahai Lotus temple in New Delhi are examples of modern temple architecture. The Dilwara temples at Mount Abu are an ecstasy in marble. Modern period has seen some beautiful Buddhist temples at Gaya from inspiration and devotion of many Buddhist countries. Many former princes of Indian states have transformed some of their forts and palaces to modern hotels which provide ancient courtly environment with modern amenities. The excellence now extends to new suburbia and new well designed cities like Chandigarh, Bhubaneshwar and Bhopal and some industrial towns like Ludhiana in the Punjab or Indore in Madhya Pradesh. Skyscrapers are appearing in many cities and villages, the best examples of which are in Mumbai, Noida, Bangalore, Hyderabad, Delhi and Gurgaon.

Rural art is flourishing and can be seen in many children's toys and pottery articles. Department of Rural Development is active in reviving many arts and crafts. District and state level fairs provide a ready outlet for creative village folk to sell their pieces direct to customers.

Indian art is now a regular feature of world renowned auctions in London and New York or in Paris. Art revival was pioneered by the Bengal artists and they have the lead in exhibiting high priced Indian arts and crafts. There has been a revolution in the depiction of the female form. Ravi Varma was the last of the classical painters. Modern style started with Jaimini Roy and is developed by F.M. Hussain and Manjit Bawa. In Delhi many markets have an art gallery and works from Jaipur, Agra, Chennai, Baroda and Kolkata are on sale and display.

Indian export potential for art products like films and canned music is tremendous and is likely to increase when dubbing of Indian films with spoken foreign languages matures. Dubbing in English and Arabic has brought very good results.

The metro, the popular conveyance of millions of Delhiites is a marvel of engineering. Metro management has invitation from so many cities of India to extend their labours to those cities. In line with the pioneering design and lay-out of the Victoria Terminus station at Mumbai, the railways are undertaking to build beautiful railway stations along the new rail routes that are being planned. A good window to Indian art and culture are the abundance of movie films made and distributed from Bollywood of Mumbai. Bollywood is second only to Hollywood in the film industry. There are movie studios in other big cities of India also specially for movies using Indian languages other than Hindi. The Indian movies are popular in many continents being a blend of opera and melodrama besides classical simplicity and modern complexity as well as dance and music.

Indian paintings now are in regular auctions all over the world. The renaissance in painting began with Rabindranath Tagore and the Tagore school but it has now spread to all corners of India. Artists of Kolkata and Jaipur and rural artists of Bihar are popular and fetch fabulous prices. Ancient centres at Mathura, Madurai and Patna are also very active.

Awakening of the Indian life has been in every sphere. Indian paintings are now in demand in the art world. In the past Indian painters were starving, but now their paintings are commanding thousands of dollars per piece in the international auctions in England or New York. A painting that an artist gave away for thirty US dollars in 1965 can now be resold for thirty thousand dollars. Art in India was patronized by the princes and it adorned their private palaces and public temples. Now it has entered the public utility places and art galleries of private individuals.

11.4 Post Modern Exports

In the era of globalization, increase of exports along with needed imports is necessary. Education and science have to be harnessed to the increased and value added production. Indian industrialization has been discussed in an earlier chapter, but much more has to be done for sustaining exports. India is now poised to participate in the post-modern exports based on new technologies, and new gains through defence preparedness. So long as there is no stable worldwide security and universal acceptance of international law for resolving issues through discussions and democratic equality, each nation has to meet aggression for some time from own resources. Nations have been plumping for nuclear weapons from their feelings of insecurity. The trading in arms is now flourishing and profitable. India is willing to enter the arms trade in a responsible manner. A supplier of arms has to be held responsible for the misuse of such arms. India is a country which has already suffered attacks from bullies of both right and left. India might be offering the following weapons and services on commercial basis. The string attached will be India's acceptance of the rights of the cause and acceptance by the purchaser, of international obligations regarding human rights. Indian supplies usually will have the assurance of supply of spares and instructions for maintenance as well as willingness to help the recipient establish repair, maintenance, and production facility with cooperation from India at his cost.

(a) *Advanced Military Hardware*

(i) Simplest and effective weapons for offence and defence are mines and radar installations. Radar warns of enemy approach and alerts defence lasers or artillery stationed in prepared positions including underground bunkers. Mines blow up communications and attacking tanks. India could also provide mines layout plans. Complying with international advice, India will not be in a position to deliver anti-personnel mines. Naval depth charges are also within the broad category of mines. Mine detection equipment is also available.

(ii) *Bombs, Ammunition, Proximity Fuses*
These are required in profusion. Best tactical doctrine could be evolved from computer simulation of the expected conflict situation. Precision guided munition and guided missiles are manufactured in India.

(b) *Computers*
India is in the forefront of computer design and in the development of computer software.
Experimental work is going on with the use of DNA chips for computer application. India is abreast of nano-technology. Indian experts have designed computer programmes designed for interconnection of merged companies.

(c) *Satellites and Satellite Support Systems*
Satellite based systems for communications, surveillance, navigation and electronic counter measures have been built. India has facilities for tracking satellites. Remote sensing and surveillance jobs can be undertaken for customers in the overall necessity of peaceful co-existence.

(d) *India has a pulsed fast reactor in operation.*

(e) *There are courses on missile technology open to selected government sponsored students.*

(f) *Aircraft*

Training is available for in flight refuelling. Transport and trainer aircraft are available for sale. Pilotless Target Aircrafat (PTA) can be supplied. India uses also engines which are designed and made in India.

(g) *Materials*

Any advanced materials are made in production development departments of Indian factories and laboratories, *e.g.* carbon fibre composites, ultra pure materials, materials for heat shields, beryllium and copper alloys, titanium coatings, titanium, iron and aluminum alloys, ceramic powder lubricants, tough paint coatings, camouflage coatings, Beta cell atomic batteries.

(h) *Sub-systems*

Electronic warfare, operational readiness indicators, anti-radiation systems, terminal homing guidance, inertial navigation system, ECM for submarines, chaff dispersion, submarine sonar, micro-fabrication technology, supersonic combustion engines for cruise missiles, surveying and satellite geodesy, electronic video recording, radiation for preservation of perishables, nuclear waste management.

Caution – A developed nation with huge investment and business in a developing country is a danger to its economy.

12 Resurgence as Part of World Development

12.1 National Resurgence

The world will remain divided in a number of nation states. World revolution began with the setting up of the UN. Resurgence of India has to be looked at as what can be achieved by a nation like India. India was in a poor shape, but the memory of the past glory was very much there and the appearance of wise leaders was providential, whose untiring efforts and adherence to policy of peace and co-existence and expressions of friendliness to all, made it possible for India to achieve a visible resurgence in all facets of civilized life. India has given an open invitation to other nations to freely draw on the Indian social and developmental experience.

12.2 National Organization

Each country has arrived at a form of national organization by its historical experience. Now that some sort of world peace has dawned, there is the opportunity for each nation to draw further from the experience of other nations and set up a better organization for itself if possible. For continued world revolution, each nation is to achieve its revolution in peace and in cooperation with other nations. The general experience is that there are no short-cuts, and the only way is to achieve revolutionary changes by democratic persuasion. The media infrastructure must remain free and democracy has to be instilled at all levels of education. The energy and talent of every individual has to be liberated and allowed to work freely towards the national resurgence. Each nation has to strike its own balance between centralization and decentralization for reaching its development goal. Indian political scene reflects our faltering progress on these lines, perhaps other nations can circumvent our mistakes and do better. The limited authority commensurate with the limited goal of any enterprise must be unfettered and assured all possible assistance, but each authority has to be held clearly accountable. This means having rule of law in every field. India gives an example of living always up to its international engagements. Even USA in spite of internal opposition is willing to get an engagement with India for development of Indian atomic energy affluence even when India has conscientious objections to signing the nuclear NPT as framed at present that seems to allow the nuclear weapon states who signed the treaty to surreptitiously proliferate.

One can ponder over the situation that at one time communism was held the acme of revolutionary philosophy. Now the communist states claim to be travelling on the road of reform to the extent they may undo the controls achieved by the dictatorship of the proletariat regimes. This is the age of democratic socialism, which was the system that attracted young Jawaharlal Nehru and also Mahatma Gandhi under his influence. The authors have not found much difference in the economics of new capitalism and new welfare state propounded by Dr. Manmohan Singh, the Prime Minister of India.

12.3 Criterion of Human Happiness

World progress will ultimately lie in the increase in the happiness of the individuals of the whole world. Half of this can be achieved by the spread of true religion of humanism and coexistence and fellow feeling of the Vaishnava variety when one can experience the pain of others. An example is of the Vaishnavite Muslim population in the villages near Jodhpur for their feelings for fauna and flora in Rajasthan. The King of Bhutan has enjoined upon his Ministers to assess their work from the increase in happiness and not in the gross national product of their charge. Besides, necessary but sufficient wealth for some minimum standard of life, the society could look at other measures that increase happiness. This requires foremost an element of security from aggression from outside and crime from within. An active and democratic security council can and would free the world from aggression by one nation on another. The required reform of UN must have priority. A Security Council for economic security can be established making welfare states legitimate and looking to the economic security of the citizens of the world and loosening the state borders for the globalization of labour. It would then be possible to encourage happiness through general recourse to religious worship and service. In the past oasis of widespread religious ardour of Hindu-Buddhism, Islam or Christianity, the spread of happiness achievable by belonging to the *sangha* like institutions ceased because of the absence of international discipline. It was scandalous to let barbarians loot and devastate India or Europe or the peaceful countries of the newly discovered America. The national governments can do much for forwarding happiness that is reached without first accumulating wealth to buy the same. In India hundreds of learned and well-bred individuals are opting for a simple life in the service of the rural people and illiterate forest dwellers. Our neighbouring countries are assisting in the pacification and autonomous democratic development of population on the borders who are now moving forward by the assistance from the rest of the nation, primarily by self help.

12.4 Education and Science

The scientific approach is not only the key to all progress, but it also is the key to intellectual satisfaction when faced with day to day problems and questions. This approach presupposes spread of learning. Mastery of sciences and engineering technologies require a planned spread of schooling, universities and institutions for various scientific specializations. India has been going on this route and is grateful to the countries of the east and the west that stretched themselves to help our nation. Industrialization is a natural corollary of development of skills and conversely multiplies the training in skills. In hoary past, India placed its teachers and intellectuals (authors and poets) on a pedestal reserved usually for gods. India's fight with superstition, bigotry and reactionary back-sliding is not yet over. The skills of science, mathematics and engineering need a lot of effort from individual aspirants. The country has every device to encourage talented young men and women to proceed with a life long effort to specialize. Incentives of social respect are often very good substitutes for wealth which is limited in a developing nation. Indian universities, medical and engineering institutions welcome foreign aspirants in a spirit of returning the gifts of education that foreign institutions have freely provided and are still giving to India.

12.5 Industrialization

Remunerative work for all adults is necessary. For a large number of people such work exists in father to son professions, family involvement in handicrafts or agriculture including pisciculture, sericulture, agriculture, and animal husbandry. In most of these activities important contribution is being made by science. Modern agriculture and related professions have become almost industrial activities. Many industries have been established for producing various inputs like fertilizers, insecticides, superior seeds, tractors and threshers, etc. There are innumerable industries based on the produce of such industries. Oils and herbs are also important for many industries. New pharmacopoeia is being built around marine products. India is demonstrating many industrial and happiness promoting products from cottage industries and rural families including new artistic creations. Modern technology contributes in important ways even to these arts and crafts.

The innovative chain needs strengthening by creating production development facilities in industry and pilot plants of every kind. A tribe of industrial consultants should exist to carry out techno-economic surveys and bring out the significance of pre-production and post-production fallouts and bye-products as well as their profitable utilization. A developing country has to strengthen the country's familiarity with electronics and electronic and optical instruments. Other fields requiring planned infrastructure are atomic energy, rocketry, aeronautics, robotics and development of communications and information media. Publication industry needs a closer look. It is languishing in most countries because there is no proper bank to give loans to publishers for printing urgently required books of international standard. The books are published and usually the authors starve. The publishers collect incentive money from authors in place of paying royalty on sales. Innovative loans for studies, house building loans or for setting up viable production are now widely available. There is great need for good medicines but the market is flooded with spurious drugs and quackery. India wants the public to take to health building routines including *yoga* and cheap herbal medicines so that there is little need for expensive treatments, but well equipped hospitals are required for reducing the havoc caused by serious malfunctioning of the human system.

Every country has to be aware of its material needs, minting its currency, catering to the needs of children for toys, for beauty aids, and kits for sports. Steel and cement are the sinews of modern life and communications. Pottery and ceramics are the first indication of development of culture. Indians made progress in many directions by the friendly assistance of other countries and would like to pay back the international debt by passing on appropriate know-how to other countries. For a number of years, cooperative development schemes for international communications, gas conduits, and production of atomic energy for civil uses are in the pipe-line, these bode well for India and for other countries.

12.6 Recreation and Tourism

Personal happiness rests on good health, stimulating exercise and entertainment. Television and telecommunications are spreading into rural and far-flung areas. Internet is expanding but needs expansion and improvement in connectivity. There ought to be liberal provision for autonomous broadcasting of radio and television signals as has been made possible for the dissemination of magazines and newspapers. Every innovative person should have access to broadcasting his contribution to those that have the urge to see or to listen. Broadcasting stations should have a local identity and short-range receiver sets could be available at a very low cost or rent.

Tourism for the well healed requires hotels, fast and secure communications and a tour operator industry. Tourism promotes awareness of culture and history. But tourism is not only for the well-to-do. India and many other countries have had tourism for the masses in the guise of pilgrimages and waiting on the saints and prophets. Fairs and bathing festivals in India have to be experienced to feel their contribution to popular awareness of existence in this world. India is a tourist paradise.

12.7 World Peace and Progress

The world has reached a stage when some international efforts for stable peace may assure its permanence. The environment for progress can be maintained so that humanity reaches its "mustopia", a whole world utopia that must be reached. Immediate necessity is to remove irritants from the consciousness of ancient failures of nations and races. Humanity can now start afresh on the strength of truth as uncovered progressively by science and on the strength of human achievements and progress in technology and skills. The world has millions of years for continued future development.

Democracy and respect for equal human rights for everyone are the means for peaceful interaction of peoples and of nations. Formulation of laws and plans could be through discussions aiming at happiness of the majority and injury to none. UN sponsored conferences would be held at many places to sort out incorporation of scientific truths in modern beliefs of mankind. All information, knowledge or skills will be imparted to all, without any discrimination, up to the limitations of their own time and capacity. The electronic and print media have to learn to maximize their communication ability. At present channels and authors waste so much effort in self or commercial glorification.

12.8 A Statement of Faith

Innumerable great men and women of the world have sanctified by blood and sacrifice the concepts of self-culture and freedom and these have to be kept alive. For a world of plenty for all there is no need for encroachment and terrorism which is only the political expression of frustration requiring redress and compromise and not excommunication from the civilized world. Resurgence of India is not a challenge but an expression of faith for the entire humanity to emerge successful in the satisfaction of their requirements and to bring about a continuous revolution towards a world of peace and plenty.

13 Terrorism and a New Turn in World Affairs

13.1 A Terror Strike 2001

In 2001 there was a major terror strike by Muslim terrorists led by Osama Bin Laden's Islamic terrorist organization when they demolished the trade towers in New York causing great havoc and anger in the USA. President Bush declared a war of vengeance against the terrorists responsible for the attack. USA discovered the links of the terrorists with Pakistan and started reviewing its policies with respect to Pakistan. Pakistan immediately declared a sympathetic war on terror in alliance with the USA. India was already suffering from terrorism arising from extremist elements in Pakistan and welcomed the resolve of USA to fight terrorism. India and USA agreed to work together against terrorism. Pakistan had reservations since it wanted to benefit from terrorism against India. Under pressure from USA and in their self-interest, India and Pakistan agreed to work together against the terrorists. Pakistan however did not realize the gravity of terrorist roots in Pakistan bordering on rebellious support for terrorism against USA, India and Israel regarded as arch enemies of Islamic regeneration. The terrorists struck against democracy in Pakistan by murdering Benazir Bhutto, the democratic winner in Pakistan and mounting severe attacks on Musharraf, the President of Pakistan to coerce him to renounce cooperation with USA . India had consistently been pursuing a policy of increasing cooperation and friendship with Pakistan which was extremely worrisome for the terrorists.

They retaliated by planning from Pakistan locations successful terror strikes on India and equally audacious like the July 2001 attack on the New York trade towers. There was an attack on the Parliament of India in December 2001 and at several locations in Mumbai, the commercial capital of India. On November 26, 2008, they attacked the famous hotel and a Jewish Centre in Mumbai killing about 180 persons including 6 Americans. This has brought about further cementing of relations between India and USA, who had already come to an agreement on nuclear energy and support to India in her quest for supply of uranium even when India is opposed to the presently formulated NPT which has not been able to restrict nuclear proliferation. India continues to woo Pakistan's cooperation in hunting terrorists and *jehadi* outfits operating from Pakistan. On the other hand Pakistan seems to continue to indulge in efforts to make deals with them at the cost of Talibanization of its northern areas including Swat region, the alleged stronghold of international Talibans inside Pakistan.

13.2 USA-India Nuclear Accord

The accord finalized in 2007 in the teeth of opposition from the Communist Party of India was a triumph of Indian democracy and the unique stability of the eleven party coalition government led by Dr. Manmohan Singh. India expects more rational trade in nuclear materials and machines bringing new prosperity to the power hungry millions of the world. With new cooperation between India and the rest of the world including USA, Russia China, Japan and Western Democracies, the drums of war will be kept at bay and there is hope for further agreements regarding disarmament, the dream of martyred Indian Prime Minister Rajiv Gandhi. The end of civil war in Sri Lanka and a possible agreement on Palestine kindle new hope of world peace. The continued friendly relations between India and Iran are also likely to help normalizing its relations with the USA, there being no serious differences between these two nations friendly to India. A free Iraq may also soon join UN. India will welcome a UN security network for whole of the world particularly against terrorism, narcotics, and possible environmental and natural hazards.

13.3 Indian Moon Shot

India successfully projected a space station that went around the moon and photographed it from all sides. Indian success has a special significance since its space science is there for all to learn and use. An Indian scientist has advanced a most plausible theory as to how Moon was built by falling meteors that could accumulate close to the earth since earth had projected a huge mass of iron explosively split from the earth's iron core that had stabilized in space close to the earth. An American scientist has discovered the evidence of a massive bundle of iron strings inside the moon which is most likely the remains of the iron mass with non-metallic inclusions from the earth. Since the piece of iron from the earth inside the moon has corners close to the moon's surface in its hemisphere closer to the earth, there is every likelihood of the iron mass inside the moon to be relatively much more accessible than the iron core from the earth's surface. There is thus an added incentive for establishing one or more mining camps on the moon in order to alleviate the growing materials crunch in the world. The world also has now more reason to get its act together for establishing a colony on the moon.

13.4 Election of Barack Obama as US President

With this election, democracy has vindicated itself as a true mirror of progress in the world. Democracy has shown that a white supremacy country of the last century can shift to the enlightened policies of equality and assured human rights. The new US President has publicly admired the progressive examples set by India in line with the ideals of the American founding fathers. To further the desirable goals set by USA and India in the world community of nations, it is necessary that peace and progress are embraced by all nations. India and Pakistan prodded also by USA are now attempting to solve together the pending problems between the two nations and to rejuvenate SAARC.

13.5 Humanist Economics

India has extended the welfare economics practiced by some countries of Europe and America to humanist economics by including certain welfare measures for its rural folk as a constitutional right. It is extending these measures within its resources to the whole country. The ambition to adopt humanist economics is practically bringing about the ambitious goal of world socialism by peaceful means following the path of democracy and assured human rights. India swears by mixed economy and coexistence to enhance happiness in the world.

13.6 Cultural Advance

There is a visible cultural advance with successful Olympic games held in China and forthcoming Commonwealth games in India. Sports and entertainment arts bring the people of the world together. All nations are now aware of this. International pilgrim and tourist traffic has expanded and is a major industry for all countries big and small. UN is in the forefront declaring many heritage sites to be preserved and kept open to tourism. Archaeology is now well documented and finds are to be placed in museums accessible to all. The nineteenth century policy of grab and cheating of less powerful countries of their heritage is now frowned upon by the entire world. One is amazed at the strong world-wide reaction to the Taliban destruction of the Bamian Buddha statues. The Hindu-Buddhism gave enlightenment to the whole world including the Hindus of those days residing around Bamian, possibly the ancestors of the present day Taliban. It is regrettable that some misguided leaders still falsify history to block enlightenment of their own people. India firmly believes that "Truth shall prevail."

13.7 Strengthening of Peace

For all nations to devote full attention to build prosperity and well-being, it is necessary that they are fully confident of their security both from internal unrest and external aggression. A nation has to heed the democratic rights of their public. Democracy can alone bring about internal security and peace. It is now fully established that democracy can bring about revolutionary changes. Only the people have to choose their representatives wisely. The external security is not possible with the tried and failed organizations depending on dictatorship of individuals or coteries. It is true that a wise king with all powers can be a good ruler for the people but sooner or later succession will give rise to instability and down right anarchy. Only democracy can solve the problems connected with the retirement of successful rulers. The UN has to be strengthened and encouraged to take on the responsibility for world-wide security and plan for the prosperous future of the whole world. The world is now manageably small in the universe open to humanity. Earth must now have a democratic governance built on the steps already being taken by the various agencies of the UN. There is need for strengthening acceptable and enforceable laws and striving for unity while preserving essentials of diversity which is necessary for future of mankind. Human mind is complex and only laws that allow reasonable co-existence of diverse views can guarantee a law abiding public. Provision for enforcement of one-world laws should be independent of national enforcement agencies, who will have only a subsidiary role. They will have, however, full authority for enforcing rule of law and for assurance of human rights for their citizens.

Index